cute & easy
crocheted cosies

cute & easy
crocheted cosies

35 simply stylish projects to make and give

Nicki Trench

CICO BOOKS

LONDON NEW YORK

Published in 2016 by CICO Books
An imprint of Ryland Peters & Small Ltd
20–21 Jockey's Fields, London WC1R 4BW

www.rylandpeters.com

10 9 8 7 6 5 4 3 2 1

Text © Nicki Trench 2016
Design, illustration and photography © CICO Books 2016

A CIP catalogue record for this book is available from the
British Library.

ISBN: 978 1 78249 321 1

Printed in China

Editor: Marie Clayton
Designer: Barbara Zuniga
Photographer: Gavin Kingcome
Stylist: Sophie Martell and Nel Haynes
Illustrator: Stephen Dew

In-house editor: Anna Galkina
Art Director: Sally Powell
Production controller: Sarah Kulasek-Boyd
Publishing Manager: Penny Craig
Publisher: Cindy Richards

Contents

introduction

Once upon a time, cosies were confined to teapots and hot water bottles, but with all the technological devices now in our households we can take much pleasure making cosies for just about anything that needs protection. In this collection there are cosies for mobile phones (pages 30 and 46), laptops (pages 32 and 40), tablets (pages 26 and 44) and eBook readers (page 34). There is a very cute Baby Cosy with a hood and ears (page 78), cafetière cosies (pages 66 and 88), a Glasses Cosy (page 106) and even a Cold Bottle Cosy (page 68) that you can take to the gym – you'll never have to worry about getting your bottle mixed up with someone else's ever again!

Devices and containers come in all different shapes and sizes, so all the patterns in this book are suggested measurements. Where possible I have given stitch multiples in the patterns, so you can adjust the size of your cosy to fit your own item. I have chosen the yarns for their yummy colours and textures – and for how easy they are to crochet with. Most cosies work well in a double knit yarn, or something even thicker for more protection, but for cosies that are purely decorative – such as the Vase Cosies on page 64 – I have a used a fine lace yarn with beautiful colours to show the light coming through the glass jars.

Most cosies are made to protect, so I have lined many of the items with a cotton fabric and used some thicker, textured stitches: a puff stitch for the Striped Laptop Cosy (page 40) and a bobble stitch for the Bobble Cafetière Cosy (page 88). If you would like the cosy even thicker you could also add some wadding between the lining and the crochet, but take care not to make the cosy too bulky. I pop my laptop into a cosy and then into my bag and – although I want it to be protected – I don't want the cosy to take up all the space (I need to keep a hook and yarn in there too!).

In this book we also have a techniques section on pages 8–23, and there are also many tips and notes to help you along when reading the patterns. One of the instructions that is used often in most of the patterns, particularly when a colour change is necessary, is: 'Cut yarn, do not fasten off'. When doing this keep the hook in the loop, cut the yarn approximately 10cm (4in) from the loop on the hook, and then join the next colour as instructed.

Once you start thinking of all the items you can cover with a crochet cosy you will get obsessed and want to crochet a cover for just about everything! I hope you have as much enjoyment making the projects in this book as I did designing them for you. Enjoy.

techniques

basic stitches

Crochet has only a few basic stitches and once you've mastered these all extended stitches follow the same principles. Practise the basic stitches before attempting your first pattern. Crochet is easy to undo because you only have one loop on the hook so you can't really go wrong. When practising keep the loops loose – you can work on creating an even tension across the fabric later.

Holding your hook and yarn

Holding the yarn and hook correctly is a very important part of crochet and once you have practised this it will help you to create your stitches at an even tension.

Holding your hook

There are two basic ways of holding the hook. I always teach the pen position as I find this more comfortable. It gives you a more relaxed arm and shoulder.

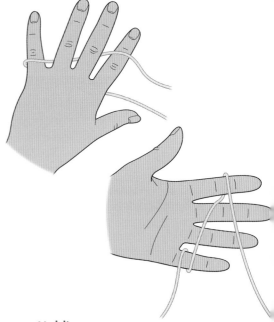

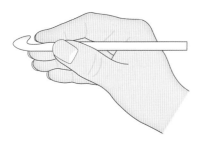

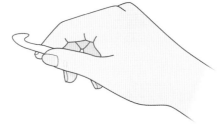

Pen position Pick up your hook as though you are picking up a pen or pencil. Keeping the hook held loosely between your fingers and thumb, turn the hook so that the tip is facing up and the hook is balanced in your hand and resting in the space between your index finger and your thumb.

Knife position But if I'm using a very large hook and chunky yarn, then I may sometimes change and use the knife position. I crochet a lot and I've learned that it's important to take care not to damage your arm or shoulder by being too tense. Make sure you're always relaxed when crocheting and take breaks.

Holding your yarn

Pick up the yarn with your little finger on the opposite hand to the hook, with palm facing towards you, the short end in front of the finger and the yarn in the crease between little finger and ring finger. Turn your hand to face downward (see above top), placing the long yarn strand on top of your index finger, under the other two fingers and wrapped right around the little finger. Then turn your hand to face you (above bottom), ready to hold the work in your middle finger and thumb.

Holding hook and yarn while crocheting

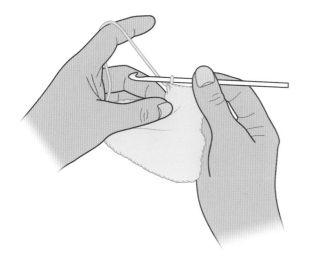

Keep your index finger, with the yarn draped over it, at a slight curve, and hold your work (or the slip knot) using the same hand, between your middle finger and your thumb and just below the crochet hook and loop/s on the hook. As you draw the loop through the hook release the yarn on the index finger to allow the loop to stay loose on the hook. If you tense your index finger, the yarn will become too tight and pull the loop on the hook too tight for you to draw the yarn through.

Holding hook and yarn for left-handers

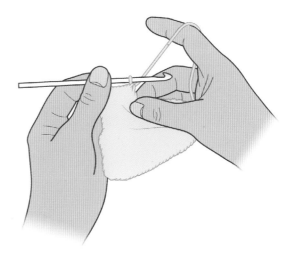

Some left-handers learn to crochet like right-handers, but others learn with everything reversed – with the hook in the left hand and the yarn in the right.

Slip knot

A slip knot is the loop that you put onto the hook to start any stitch in crochet.

1 Make a circle of yarn as shown.

2 In one hand hold the circle at the top where the yarn crosses, and let the tail drop down at the back so that it falls across the centre of the loop. With your free hand or the tip of a crochet hook, pull a loop through the circle.

3 This forms a very loose loop on the hook.

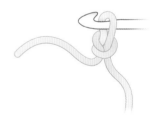

4 Pull both yarn ends gently to tighten the loop around the crochet hook shank.

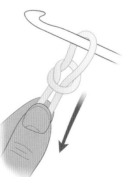

5 Make sure the loop is not TOO tight. It needs to slip easily along the shank.

Chain stitches
(abbreviated ch)

Chains are the basis of all crochet. This is the stitch you have to practise first because you need to make a length of chains to be able to make the first row or round of any other stitch. Practising these will also give you the chance to get used to holding the hook and the yarn correctly.

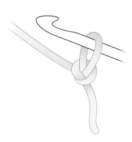

1 Start with the tip of the hook pointed upwards, with the slip knot on your hook sitting loosely so there is enough gap to pull a strand of yarn through the loop on the hook.

2 Catch the yarn with the hook, circling it around the strand of yarn.

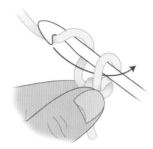

3 As you catch the yarn, turn the tip of the hook downwards, holding the knot immediately under the loop on the hook with your left hand between finger and thumb.

4 Then gently pull the strand of yarn through the loop on the hook. As soon as the tip of the hook comes through the loop, turn the tip of the hook immediately upwards.

Chain space
[abbreviated ch sp]

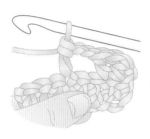

1 A chain space is the space that has been made under a chain in the previous round or row and falls in between other stitches.

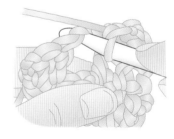

2 Stitches into a chain space are made directly into the hole created under the chain and not into the chain stitches themselves.

Slip stitch
(abbreviated ss)

A slip stitch is the shortest crochet stitch and is usually worked into other stitches rather than into a foundation chain, because it is rarely used to make a whole piece of crochet. It is mainly used to join rounds or to take the yarn neatly along the tops of stitches to get to a certain point without having to fasten off. It can also be used as a joining stitch.

1 To make a slip stitch, first insert the hook through the stitch (chain or chain space). Then wrap the yarn round the hook.

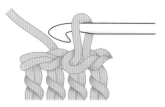

2 Pull the yarn through both the stitch (chain or chain space) and the loop on the hook at the same time, so you will be left with one loop on the hook.

Double crochet
(abbreviated dc)

Double crochet is the most commonly used stitch of all. It makes a firm tight crochet fabric. If you are just starting out, it is the best stitch to start with because it is the easiest to make.

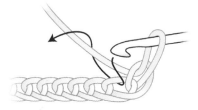

1 Make a foundation chain, then insert the tip of the hook into the 2nd chain from the hook. Catch the yarn with the hook by taking the hook around the back of the yarn strand. Pull the yarn through the chain only, with the hook pointed downwards. As soon as you have brought the yarn through, immediately turn the hook upwards – this will help to keep the loop on the hook and prevent it sliding off. Keep the hook in a horizontal position.

2 You will now have two loops on the hook. Wrap the yarn round the hook again (with the hook sitting at the front of the yarn), turn the hook to face downwards and pull the yarn through the two loops, turning the hook to point upwards as soon as you have pulled the yarn through.

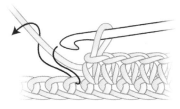

3 One loop is now left on the hook. Keep the hook pointed upwards (this is the default position of the hook until you start the next stitch). Continue working one double crochet into each chain to the end of the foundation chain.

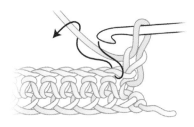

4 Turn the work to begin the next row. Make one chain and work the first double crochet into the top of the first double crochet in the row below (picking up the two loops at the top of the stitch). Work one double crochet into each double crochet stitch in the row below, to the end of the row.

5 For all subsequent rows, repeat Step 4.

Half treble
(abbreviated htr)

Half trebles are stitches that are the next height up from a double crochet stitch. The yarn is wrapped around the hook first before going into the stitch (or space) and then once pulled through the stitch (or space) there will be three loops on the hook. The middle loop is from the strand that was wrapped around the hook. Before you attempt to pull the yarn through all three stitches, make sure the loops sit straight and loosely on the hook so that you can pull another strand through to complete the stitch.

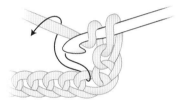

1 Make your foundation chain as usual to start. Before inserting the hook into the work, wrap the yarn round the hook. Then with the yarn wrapped around the hook, insert the hook through the 3rd chain from the hook. Work 'yarn round hook' again (as shown by the arrow).

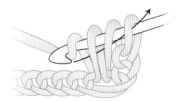

2 Pull the yarn through the chain. You now have three loops on the hook. Yarn round hook again and pull it through all three loops on the hook.

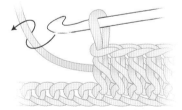

3 You will be left with one loop on the hook. Continue working one half treble into each chain to the end of the foundation chain.

first half treble of row

4 Turn the work to begin the next row. Make two chains. Work one half treble into each half treble stitch in the row below to the end of the row.

5 For all subsequent rows, repeat Step 4.

Treble
(abbreviated tr)

A treble is a very common stitch; it gives a more open fabric than a double crochet or a half treble, which both give a denser fabric, and it's a one step taller stitch than a half treble. As with the half treble, the yarn is wrapped around the hook first before going into the stitch (or space) and then, once pulled through the stitch, there are three loops on the hook. The middle loop is from the strand that was wrapped around the hook. Before you attempt to pull the yarn through the next two stitches on the hook, make sure the loops sit straight and loosely on the hook so that you will be able to pull another strand through to complete the stitch.

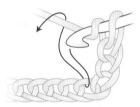

1 Before inserting the hook into the work, wrap the yarn round the hook. Then with the yarn wrapped around the hook, insert the hook through the 4th chain from the hook. Work 'yarn round hook' again (as shown by the arrow).

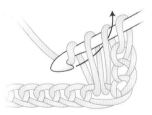

2 Pull the yarn through the chain. You now have three loops on the hook. Yarn round hook again and pull it through the first two loops on the hook.

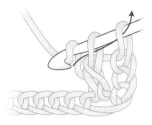

3 You now have two loops on the hook. Yarn round hook again and pull it through the two remaining loops.

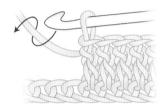

4 You will be left with one loop on the hook. Continue working one treble into each chain to the end of the foundation chain.

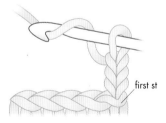

first st

5 Turn the work to begin the next row. Make three chains. Work one treble into each treble stitch in the row below to the end of the row.

6 For all subsequent rows, repeat Step 5.

Double treble
(abbreviated dtr)

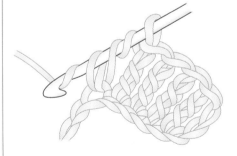

Yarn around hook twice, insert hook into the stitch, yarn around hook, pull a loop through (four loops on hook), yarn around hook, pull the yarn through two stitches (three loops on hook), yarn around hook, pull a loop through the next two stitches (two loops on hook), yarn around hook, pull a loop through the last two stitches.

Where to insert the hook in your crochet

One of the tricks of learning how to crochet is to understand clearly where to insert the hook to make a stitch, whether into a chain, a space in the crochet or into stitches in the row or round below.

The general rule for working into the stitch below to make a new stitch is to pick up both the top loops of the stitch – that means you will usually be inserting your hook under the two loops at the top of the stitch that look like a 'V'. However, you may be instructed in the pattern to pick up either only the front or only the back loop of the stitch, which gives the crochet a different 'look' or texture.

Working into top of stitch

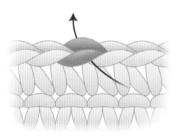

Unless otherwise directed the hook will be inserted into a stitch under both of the two loops on the top of the stitch. This is the standard technique.

Working into front loop of top of stitch

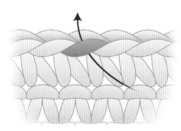

To pick up the front loop of the stitch, pick up the front loop from underneath at the front of the work.

Working into back loop of top of stitch

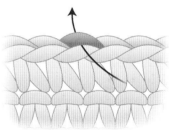

To pick up the back loop of the stitch, insert the hook between the front and the back loop, picking up the back loop from the front of the work.

lining crochet pieces

Method 1

1 Press and block the crochet piece, then measure it. Press the lining to make sure there are no creases. Cut out the fabric lining to fit the crocheted piece, allowing an extra 2.5cm (1in) around each edge for hems. For example, if the crocheted piece measures 28 x 21.5cm (11 x 8½in), cut out a piece of fabric 33 x 26.5cm (13 x 10½in).

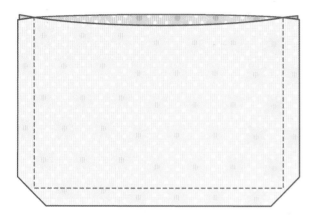

2 Place the two lining pieces with RS together. Pin and sew the side seams, and the bottom seam is there is one, ensuring that the lining is exactly the same measurement, at the sides, as the crochet piece. Trim across the corners. Do not turn RS out.

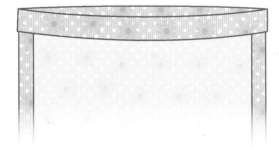

3 Fold the top edge of lining to the outside by 2.5cm (1in) and press in place.

4 Make up the crochet piece and turn RS out. Insert the lining into the crochet piece, so WS are together. Ease the lining right down inside the crochet piece, so it fits nicely at the bottom. Using long plastic or glass-headed pins, pin the lining to the crochet piece around the opening; start pinning at the side seams, then pin the centre (half way) of each side, then pin in between the centre pin and the side seam pin. Add more pins if necessary to ensure it's neatly pinned all round.

5 If adding a ribbon tie, cut the ribbon in half or to the desired length. Insert one end of the ribbon at the centre top in between the lining and the crochet piece – you may need to take out a pin to do this. Pin the ribbon in position and repeat on the other side.

6 Using a sewing needle and thread, slip stitch the lining and crochet piece together along the top edge, securing the ribbon at the same time, if adding. Trim the ends of the ribbon to neaten the edges if necessary.

7 Add two or three hand stitches in sewing thread on each side of the bottom edges to secure the lining to the crochet piece and keep it in position.

Method 2

If the crocheted piece must be lined before it is made up (particularly if it has a flap), follow Step 1 (above left) but allow only 1cm (½in) extra around each edge for the seams. Place the lining on top of the crocheted piece with WS together. Then fold the lining piece 1cm (½in) over to the wrong side all round and pin the folded edge to the crochet. Using a sewing needle and thread, sew the lining to the crocheted piece with hand stitches. Fold the crochet piece with RS together or as instructed in the pattern, then sew the seams of the crocheted piece using yarn and a yarn sewing needle. Turn RS out.

chapter one

cosy tech

striped wave iPad cover

We all love our iPads and you'll love yours even more with its own unique cover. The stripes and waves look bright and cheerful and you can fit the iPad inside either with or without its hard cover.

materials

Louisa Harding Cassia, 75% superwash wool/25% nylon DK weight yarn

1 x 50g (1¾oz) ball – approx. 132m (144yd) – each of:
A: 102 Ecru (off white)
B: 115 Lipstick (pink)
C: 108 Lime (green)

3.5mm (US size E/4) crochet hook

1m (40in) of 7mm (⅜in) wide ribbon

33 x 26.5cm (13 x 10½in) of cotton lining fabric, allowing for an approx. 2.5cm (1in) seam allowance on all sides

Hand sewing needle and thread to match lining

tension

23 sts x 9 rows over a 10cm (4in) square, working Wave pattern using 3.5mm (US size E/4) hook and Louisa Harding Cassia yarn.

finished measurement

Approx. 28 x 21.5cm (11 x 8½in) to fit a standard iPad

note

The multiple is 10 sts + 3 sts (see page 18).

abbreviations

approx. approximate(ly)
ch chain
cont continu(e)(ing)
dc double crochet
htr half treble
rep repeat
RS right side
st(s) stitch(es)
ss slip stitch
tr treble
tr3tog treble crochet 3 stitches together
WS wrong side
yrh yarn round hook

colourway

Work the cover in a repeating stripe sequence of 2 rows A, 2 rows B, 2 rows C.

• •

cover

(made in one piece)
Foundation chain: Using A, make 43ch.
Row 1: Cont with A, 1tr in third ch from hook, 1tr in each of next 3 ch, tr3tog over next 3 ch, 1tr in each of next 3 ch, *3tr in next ch, 1tr in each of next 3 ch, tr3tog over next 3 ch, 1tr in each of next 3 ch; rep from * to last ch, 2tr in last ch.

tips

Make sure that you go into the first st at the beginning and end of the rows, and make the 2 trebles into the top of the 3rd chain from the previous row.

When at the end of each 2-row colour sequence, cut off the yarn but do not fasten off, then join in new colour.

Row 2: Cont in colour sequence, 3ch, 1tr in each of first 4 sts, tr3tog over next 3 sts, 1tr in each of next 3 sts, *3tr in next st, 1tr in each of next 3 sts, tr3tog over next 3 sts, 1tr in each of next 3 sts; rep from * to end, 2tr in top of 3-ch at end of row.

Rep Row 2, changing colour every 2 rows until work measures approximately 28cm (11in).

Fasten off.

edging 1:

Cont with same colour, 1ch, 1dc in first st, 1dc in next st, [1htr in each of next 2 sts, 1tr in each of next 3 sts, 1htr in each of next 2 sts, 1dc in each of next 3 sts] four times. Fasten off.

edging 2:

Working on underside of Foundation chain, join A on RS in top of last treble at start of Row 1.

3ch, 1tr in first ch, [1htr in each of next 2 ch, 1dc in each of next 3 ch, 1htr in each of next 2 ch, 1tr in each of next 3 ch] four times. Fasten off.

finishing

Block Cover if necessary and sew in ends.

With RS together, join side and bottom seams.

Make and insert lining and ribbon for ties at top edge, following instructions on page 22, Method 1.

key

⬭	**ch** chain
⊤	**tr** treble
⋀	**tr3tog** treble crochet 3 stitches together
⋁	**3tr** 3 treble crochet stitches in one stitch
▶	starting pointer
▷	ending pointer

wave stitch chart

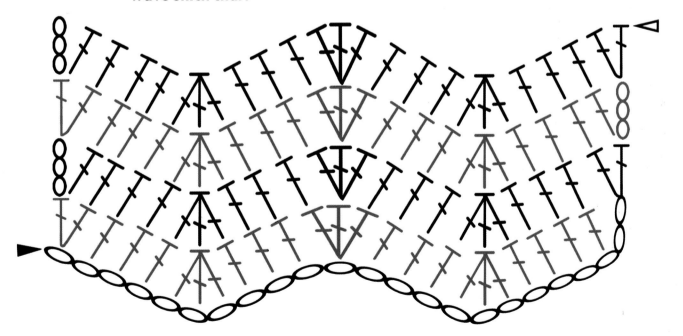

mobile phone cosies

This is a great project for a beginner; quick to make using a basic double crochet stitch and decorated with a picot edge and flower. It makes a really great gift and can be made in no time, and for any size phone.

materials

Louisa Harding Cassia, 75% superwash wool/25% nylon DK weight yarn

1 x 50g (1¾oz) ball – approx. 132m (144yd) – each of:

cosy
A: 103 Chick (yellow)
     105 Glacier (pale blue)
     104 Powder (pale pink)
     112 Prince (dark blue)

flowers
B: 115 Lipstick (bright pink)

french knot
C: 102 Ecru (off white)

3mm (US size D/3) crochet hook

3.5mm (US size E/4) crochet hook

tension

20 sts x 22 rows over 10cm (4in) square,
working double crochet using 3.5mm
(US size E/4) hook and Louisa Harding
Cassia yarn.

finished measurement

Approx. 12.5cm (5in) long x 7cm (2¾in)
wide, to fit an iPhone 5, approx: 12.5cm (5in)
high, 6cm (2¼in) wide

note

The multiple is any number of sts (+ 1 for
the base ch) (see page 18).

abbreviations

approx. approximate(ly)
ch chain
dc double crochet
rep repeat
RS right side
st(s) stitch(es)
ss slip stitch
WS wrong side

cosy

Row 1: Using 3.5mm (US size E/4) crochet
hook and A, make 15ch, 1dc in second ch
from hook, 1dc in each ch to end. (14 sts)
Row 2: 1ch, 1dc in each st. (14 sts)
Rep Row 2 until work measures approx. 25.5cm (10in) – 55 rows,
or twice length of device – finishing with a WS row. Do not fasten
off.

picot edge:
Next row (RS): *3ch, ss in first of 3-ch, miss next st, 1dc in each
of next 2 sts; rep from * to end, ending last repeat with 1dc in last
2 sts, 3ch, ss in first of 3-ch, miss next st, 1dc in last st. (5 picots)
Fasten off.
Join yarn on RS at other end of piece (start of Row 1). Working on
underside of foundation ch, *3ch, ss in first of 3-ch, miss next ch,
1dc in each of next 2 ch; rep from * to end, ending last rep with
1dc in last 2-ch, 3ch, ss in first of 3-ch, miss next st, 1dc in last ch.
(5 picots).
Fasten off.

flowers

(make 1 per Cosy)
Using 3mm (US size D/3) crochet hook and B, make 4ch, join with
a ss in first ch to form a ring.
Round 1 (RS): [5ch, 1ss in ring] 5 times. (5 petals)
Fasten off.
Using C, make a French knot in the centre.

finishing

Fold Cosy lengthways with RS together. Pin and sew side seams.
Block and press.
Turn RS out.
Sew Flower onto centre on RS of Cosy.

patchwork laptop cover

A great piece of patchwork to show off and protect your laptop – make as many squares as you need to cover the size. Here I've used the colours in Debbie Bliss Baby Cashmerino, because the shades are very on-trend and it feels very soft to carry around.

materials

Debbie Bliss Baby Cashmerino, 55% wool/33% acrylic/ 12% cashmere lightweight DK (sport weight) yarn 50g (1¾oz) balls – approx. 125m (137yd) per ball – of:

squares

1 ball each of:
700 Ruby (red)
202 Light blue (pale blue)
94 Rose pink (pale pink)
03 Mint (pale green)
84 Toffee (bronze)
91 Acid yellow (yellow)
101 Ecru (off white)
65 Clotted cream (cream)
204 Baby blue (mid blue)
57 Mist (grey)

top edging

1 ball of:
202 Light Blue (pale blue)

2.5mm (US size C/2) crochet hook – or size needed to make a 4.5cm (1¾in) square

2 pieces of lining fabric, each approx. 45 x 35cm (18 x 14in)

1m (1yd) of 2.5cm (1in) wide ribbon

Large snap fastener approx. 2cm (¾in) diameter

tension

Each square measures approx. 4.5cm (1¾in).

finished measurement

Approx. 40cm (15¾in) wide x 30cm (12in) long, to fit a Macbook Pro measuring 36.5cm (14½in) wide x 25cm (10in) long x 1cm (½in) deep

abbreviations

alt alternate
approx. approximate(ly)
ch chain
dc double crochet
foll following
htr half treble
rep repeat
RS right side
sp space
ss slip stitch
st(s) stitch(es)
tr treble

colourway

Make total of 126 squares in the following colours:
Red x 14
Pale blue x 14
Pale pink x 14
Pale green x 14
Bronze x 14
Yellow x 14
Off white x 13
Cream x 12
Mid blue x 10
Grey x 7

square

Make 4ch, join with a ss to form a ring.

Round 1 (RS): 1ch, 12dc in ring, join with a ss in first dc. (12 sts)

Round 2: 3ch (counts as first tr), 1tr in same st, 2tr in each st to end, join with a ss in first tr. (24 sts)

Round 3: 3ch (counts as 1tr), 2tr in same st (first corner), 1htr in next st, 1dc in each of next 3 sts, 1htr in next st. *3tr in next st (second corner), 1htr in next st, 1dc in each of next 3 sts, 1htr in next st; rep from * twice more (four corners), join with a ss in top of first 3-ch. Fasten off.

finishing

Block and press Squares.

Set out Front with 9 Squares across (width) x 7 down (length), with the colours evenly spaced and with squares RS facing up.

Join in strips with RS together, first vertically then horizontally, using a neutral colour yarn. Press.

Rep for back.

With RS together, join sides and bottom seams of front and back, leaving top open. Turn RS out.

top edging

With RS facing, join A in a st to side of one seam. 1ch, 1dc in same st, 1dc in next and each st around top to end, join with a ss in first dc.

Fasten off.

Make and insert lining following instructions on page 22, Method 1. Attach edging ribbon at top edge of lining before slip stitching crochet and lining together.

kindle cosy

This Kindle cosy is made using a bobble stitch, which makes a lovely texture and gives a good thickness to keep the Kindle protected. Here I've used a lovely Dorset button to match the yarn colour and lining.

materials

Debbie Bliss Baby Cashmerino, 55% wool/33% acrylic/12% cashmere lightweight DK (sport weight) yarn
2 x 50g (1¾oz) balls - approx. 250m (274yd) of:
68 Peach Melba

3mm (US size D/3) crochet hook

Approx. 25.5cm (10¼in) square of cotton lining fabric

Sewing needle and thread

Button

Snap fastener

tension

Approx. 9 bobbles x 10 bobble rows over 10cm (4in) square, using 3mm (US size D/3) hook and Debbie Bliss Baby Cashmerino.

finished measurement

To fit a Kindle 17 x 11.5 x 1.5cm (6¾ x 4½ x ½in), cosy measures approx. 19 x 14.75cm (7½ x 5¾in)

note

The multiple is 4 sts + 3 sts (+ 1 for the base ch) (see page 18).

abbreviations

approx. approximate(ly)
ch chain
dc double crochet
rep repeat
RS right side
ss slip stitch
st(s) stitch(es)
tr treble
WS wrong side
yrh yarn round hook

special abbreviation

5trCL 5 treble cluster/bobble – yrh, insert hook in st, yrh, pull yarn through work (3 loops on hook). Yrh, pull yarn through first 2 loops on hook (2 loops on hook). Yrh, insert hook in same st, yrh, pull yarn through work (4 loops on hook), yrh, pull yarn through first 2 loops on hook (3 loops left on hook). Yrh, insert hook in same st, yrh, pull yarn through work (5 loops on hook), yrh, pull yarn through first 2 loops on hook (4 loops left on hook). Yrh, insert hook in same st, yrh, pull yarn through work (6 loops on hook), yrh, pull yarn through first 2 loops on hook (5 loops left on hook). Yrh, insert hook in same st, yrh, pull yarn through work (7 loops on hook), yrh, pull yarn through first 2 loops on hook (6 loops left on hook). Yrh, pull yarn through all 6 loops on hook (1 loop left on hook). Make 1ch to complete 5trCL.

tip

When working a double crochet into the top of the 5-treble cluster, make the double crochet stitch into the chain at the top of the cluster.

main piece

Row 1 (RS): Make 28ch, 1dc in second ch from hook, 1dc in each ch to end. (27 sts)

Begin bobble pattern

Row 2 (WS): 1ch, *1dc in each of first 3 dc, 5trCL in next dc; rep from * to last 3 sts, 1dc in each of last 3 dc. (6 bobbles)

Row 3: 1ch, *1dc in each of next 3 dc, 1dc in top of next 5trCL; rep from * to last 3 sts, 1dc in each of last 3 dc.

Row 4: 1ch, 1dc in first dc, 5trCL in next dc, *1dc in each of next 3 dc, 5trCL in next dc; rep from * to last st, 1dc in last dc. (7 bobbles)

Row 5: 1ch, 1dc in first dc, *1dc in top of next 5trCL, 1dc in each of next 3 dc; rep from * to last 5trCL, 1dc in top of last 5trCL, 1dc in last dc.

Rep Rows 2-5 until 37 bobble rows have been worked or work measures approx. 38cm (15in) ending on a Row 5.

Fasten off.

tab

Row 1: Make 8ch, 1dc in second ch from hook, 1dc in each ch to end. (7 sts)

Row 2: 1ch, 1dc in each st to end. (7 sts)

Rep Row 2 until tab measures approx. 9cm (3½in).
Fasten off.

finishing

Pin and block Tab.

With RS together join side seams of Main Piece, leaving top open. Turn RS out.

Make and insert lining for the Main Piece (see page 22, Method 1), and line the Tab following Method 2. Pin along top edge of Main Piece and insert Tab between lining and crochet piece, with WS of Tab facing WS of lining, approx. 2.5cm (1in) down into lining on one side only. Hand sew lining to crochet piece using cotton thread around top of lining, incorporating one end of Tab.

Sew button onto RS of Tab at end that flaps over onto other side of crochet piece. Sew one side of snap fastener to Tab lining underneath button. Sew other side of snap fastener onto main crochet piece to match.

iPod cosy

A pretty drawstring cosy to pop onto your iPod to protect it while it's in your handbag, made using a 4ply yarn with a pretty lace edging.

materials

Fyberspates Scrumptious 4ply, 55% superwash merino wool, 45% silk 4ply yarn
1 x 100g hank – approx. 365m (399yd) – of
A: 318 Glisten (pale grey)

Debbie Bliss Rialto Lace, 100% extra fine merino laceweight yarn
1 x 50g (1¾oz) ball – approx. 390m (427yd) – of:
B: 035 Acid Yellow (yellow-green)

2.5mm (US size C/2) crochet hook

Approx. 50cm (20in) of 5mm (¼in) wide ribbon

tension

Approx. 26 sts x 32 rows over 10cm (4in) square working double crochet using 2.5mm (US size C/2) hook and Fyberspates Scrumptious 4ply yarn.

finished measurement

To fit an iPod Touch, approx: 13cm (5in) high, 6cm (2⅜in) wide

note

The multiple for the cosy is any number of sts (+ 1 for the base ch).
The multiple for the edging is 12 sts + 2 sts (see page 18).

abbreviations

approx. approximate(ly)
ch chain
ch sp chain space
dc double crochet
rep repeat
RS right side
sp space
st(s) stitch(es)
tr treble
WS wrong side

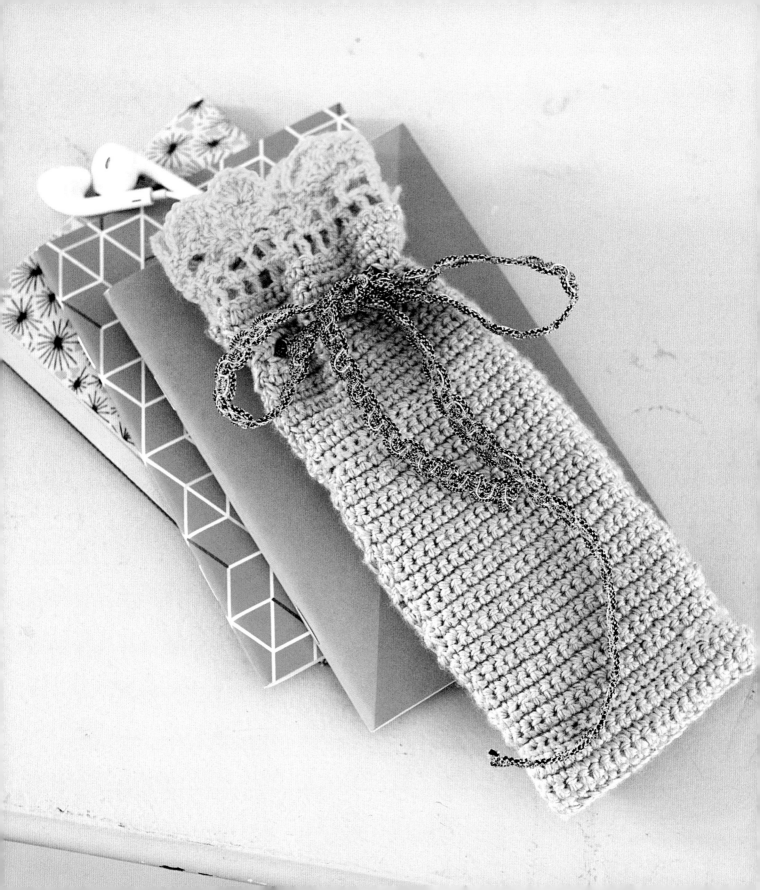

cosy

(make two, Front and Back)

Row 1: Using A, make 21ch, 1dc in second ch from hook, 1dc in each ch to end. (20 sts)

Rows 2-4: 1ch, 1dc in each st to end. (20 sts)
Cut yarn, do not fasten off.

Rows 5-6: Join B, 1ch, 1dc in each st to end. (20 sts)
Cut yarn, do not fasten off.

Row 7: Join A, 1ch, 1dc in each st to end. (20 sts)
Rep Row 7 until work measures 11.5cm (4½in), ending on a WS Row.
Cut yarn, do not fasten off.

Next 2 rows: Join B, 1ch, 1dc in each st to end. (20 sts)

Next 11 rows: Join A, 1ch, 1dc in each st to end.

make ribbon holes:

Next row: 1ch, 1dc in first st, 2ch, miss next 2 sts, *1dc in each of next 2 sts, 2ch, miss next 2 sts; rep from * to end, 1dc in last st.

Next row: 1ch, 2dc in first st, 2dc in next ch sp, *1dc in each of next 2 sts, 2dc in next ch sp; rep from * to last st, 2dc in last st. (22 sts)

Next 2 Rows: 1ch, 1dc in each st to end. (22 sts)

Next Row: 1ch, 2dc in first st, 1dc in each st to last st, 2dc in last st. (24 sts)
Cut yarn, do not fasten off.

edging:

Row 1 (RS): Join B, 3ch (counts as 1tr), 1tr in first st, 1ch, *miss next st, [1tr, 1ch] in next st; rep from * to last 2 sts, 1tr in each of last 2 sts. (14 tr)

Row 2:
1ch, 1dc in first st,
2ch, [miss next tr, next ch sp], 1tr in next tr,
2ch, [miss next ch sp, next tr], 1tr in next ch sp,
2ch, [miss next tr, next ch sp], 1tr in next tr,
2ch, [miss next ch sp, next tr], 1dc in next ch sp,
2ch, [miss next tr, next ch sp], 1tr in next tr,
2ch, [miss next ch sp, next tr], 1tr in next ch sp,
2ch, [miss next tr, next ch sp], 1tr in next tr,
2ch, [miss next ch sp, next tr], 1dc in top of 3-ch from previous row.

Row 3:
1ch, 1dc in first st,
2ch, miss next ch sp, 1dc in next st,
2ch, miss next ch sp, [1tr, 1ch in next st] twice, 1tr in same st,
[2ch, miss next ch sp, 1dc in next st] three times,
2ch, miss next ch sp, [1tr, 1ch in next st] twice, 1tr in same st,
2ch, miss next ch sp, 1dc in next st,
2ch, miss next ch sp, 1dc in last st.

Row 4:
4ch, [miss first ch sp, miss next dc, miss next ch sp], 1tr in next tr,
3tr in next ch sp, 1ch, miss next tr,
3tr in next ch sp, 1tr in next tr,
1ch, [miss next ch sp, miss next dc, miss next ch sp], 1tr in next dc, 1ch,
[miss next ch sp, miss next dc, miss next ch sp], 1tr in next tr,
3tr in next ch sp, 1ch, miss next tr,
3tr in next ch sp, 1tr in next tr,
[miss next ch sp, miss next dc, miss next ch sp],
1tr in last dc.

Row 5:
1ch, miss first tr, 1dc in next tr,
miss next tr, 7tr in next tr, miss next tr, 1dc in next ch sp,
miss next tr, 7tr in next tr, miss next tr, 1dc in next tr,
miss next ch sp, 7tr in next tr,
miss next ch sp, 1dc in next tr,
miss next tr, 7tr in next tr,
miss next tr, 1dc in next ch sp,
miss next tr, 7tr in next tr,
miss next tr, 1dc in next tr, 1dc in 3rd of 4-ch.
Fasten off.

finishing

With RS together join side and bottom seams.

Thread ribbon through ribbon holes and pull ribbon to close once iPod is inside.

striped laptop cosy

This is made using puff stitch, a lovely thick stitch that will keep the laptop protected. It's very colourful, with bright stripes and a ribbon tie.

materials

Louisa Harding Cassia, 75% superwash wool/25% nylon DK weight yarn

1 x 50g (1¾oz) ball - approx. 132m (144yd) - each of:

A: 112 Prince (mid blue)
B: 108 Lime (green)
C: 104 Powder (pale pink)
D: 111 Earth (brown)
E: 103 Chick (yellow)
F: 105 Glacier (pale blue)
G: 115 Lipstick (bright pink)
H: 101 White (white)

3.5mm (US size E/4) crochet hook

Piece of cotton lining fabric size of laptop, plus 1.5cm (⅝in) all round for top, side and bottom seams.

Approx. 1m (1yd) pink ribbon

tension

10 Puff stitches and 8 rows over 10cm (4in) square, using 3.5mm (US size E/4) hook and Louisa Harding Cassia yarn.

finished measurement

Approx. 33cm (13in) wide x 27cm (10½in) long, to fit a Macbook Air measuring 30cm (12in) wide x 19cm (7½in) long.

abbreviations

approx. approximate(ly)
ch chain
cont continu(e)(ing)
dc double crochet
rep repeat
RS right side
sp space
ss slip stitch
sp space
st(s) stitch(es)
tr treble
yrh yarn round hook

special abbreviation

3tr-Puff 3 treble puff stitch - [yrh and insert hook into st, yrh and pull loop up to tr height] three times, yrh, pull through all loops on hook.

note

The multiple is 4 sts + 3 sts (+ 1 for the base ch) (see page 18).

cosy

Using A, make 72ch.

Row 1: 1dc in second ch from hook, 1dc in each ch to end. (71 sts)

Rows 2–3: 1ch, 1dc in each st to end. (71 sts)

Row 4: 1ch, 1dc in first st, [3tr-Puff, 2ch, 3tr-Puff] in next st, *miss 3 sts, [3tr-Puff, 2ch, 3tr-Puff] in next st; rep from * to last st, 1dc in last st. Cut yarn A, do not fasten off.

Row 5: Join B, 1ch, 1dc in first st, [3tr-Puff, 2ch, 3tr-Puff] in first 2-ch sp, *miss 2 Puffs, [3tr-Puff, 2ch, 3tr-Puff] into next 2-ch sp; rep from * ending 1dc in last dc. Cut yarn, do not fasten off.

Rep Row 5, changing colours in sequence A, B, C, D, E, F, G, H until approx. 25cm (10in) or 24 Puff Rows have been worked, ending with A.

Do not fasten off.

top edge:

Next row: 1ch, 1dc in top of first Puff, 2dc in next 2-ch (in centre of 2 Puffs), 1dc in top of next Puff, *1dc in top of next Puff, 2dc in next 2-ch, 1dc in top of next Puff; rep from * until end. (71 sts)

Next 2 rows: 1ch, 1dc in each st to end. (71 sts)

Fasten off.

finishing

Sew in ends. With RS together fold Cosy in half widthways and sew up side and bottom seams.

Make a lining incorporating ribbon ties (see page 22, Method 1). Insert lining into Cosy with WS together. Turn over the hem of the lining at the top edge and pin in place around the edge of the crochet piece. Hand sew edge in place.

iPad cosy with flap

A bright and cheerful iPad cosy that will hold an iPad in its hard cover and give it added protection. This makes a great present for the man in your life.

materials

Debbie Bliss Rialto DK, 100% merino wool DK weight yarn
1 x 50g (1¾oz) ball – approx. 105m (115yd) – each of:
A: 70 Pool (blue)
C: 45 Gold (yellow)
D: 12 Scarlet (red)

Louisa Harding Cassia, 75% superwash wool/25% nylon DK weight yarn
1 x 50g (1¾oz) ball – approx. 132m (144yd) – of:
B: 113 Silver (grey)

3.5mm (US size E/4) crochet hook

1 button

20 x 30cm (8 x 12in) pieces x 2 of cotton lining fabric for the sides

20 x 20cm (8 x 8in) piece of cotton lining fabric for the flap

Hand sewing needle and thread to match lining

tension

21 sts x 22 rows over a 10cm (4in) square, working double crochet using 3.5mm (US size E/4) hook and Debbie Bliss Rialto DK yarn.

finished measurement

Approx. 27.5 x 20cm (11 x 8in), to fit a standard iPad in its hard cover

note

The multiple is any number of sts (+ 1 for the base ch) (see page 18).

abbreviations

approx. approximate(ly)
ch chain
dc double crochet
dc2tog double crochet 2 stitches together
rep repeat
RS right side
st(s) stitch(es)
ss slip stitch

• •

cosy

Made in one piece, starting at top edge of one side and finishing at top edge of other side.
Row 1 (RS): Using A, make 39ch, 1dc in second ch from hook, 1dc in each ch to end. (38 sts)
Next 4 Rows: 1ch, 1dc in each st to end. (38 sts)
Cut yarn, do not fasten off. Join B.
Next 17 Rows: Using B, 1dc in each st to end.
Cut yarn, do not fasten off. Join C.
Next 37 Rows: Using C, 1dc in each st to end.
Cut yarn, do not fasten off.
Next 8 Rows: Using A, 1dc in each st to end.
Cut yarn, do not fasten off.
Next 37 Rows: Using C, 1dc in each st to end.
Cut yarn, do not fasten off.

Next 17 Rows: Using B, 1dc in each st to end.
Cut yarn, do not fasten off.
Next 4 Rows: Using A, 1dc in each st to end.
Cut yarn, do not fasten off. Join D.

flap:
Rows 1–7: Using D, 1ch, 1dc in each st to end. (38 sts)
Row 8: 1ch, dc2tog, 1dc in each st to last 2 sts, dc2tog. (36 sts)
Rep last two rows until 18 sts remain, then rep Row 8 until
4 sts remain.
Next Row: [Dc2tog] twice. (2 sts)
Next Row: Dc2tog.
Do not fasten off.

button loop:
Make 8ch, join with a ss in top of last dc2tog.
Fasten off.

finishing
Sew in ends. Block and press.

Line crochet piece on WS (before sewing seams) – see page 22,
Method 2 for lining instructions.

With RS together, fold bottom edge to match first row of Flap. Pin
side seams and sew.
Turn RS out. Attach button on RS of front to match Button loop.

striped phone cosy

This cosy fits a larger mobile phone, and is nice and bright and easy to find in a bag! Here I've used Baby Cashmerino yarn as I love the colours, but this is a perfect project for using up scraps as it requires very little yarn.

materials

Debbie Bliss Baby Cashmerino, 55% wool/33% acrylic/12% cashmere lightweight DK (sport weight) yarn
1 x 50g (1¾oz) balls – approx. 125m (137yd) – each of:
A: 68 Peach Melba (peach)
B: 59 Mallard (dark blue)
C: 02 Apple (light green)
D: 101 Ecru (off white)
E: 06 Candy Pink (pink)
F: 202 Light Blue (light blue)
G: 34 Red (red)
H: 90 Leaf (dark green)

3mm (US size D/3) crochet hook

tension

20 sts x 24 rows over a 10cm (4in) square, working double crochet using 3mm (US size D/3) hook and Debbie Bliss Baby Cashmerino yarn.

finished measurement

Approx. 9 x 15cm (3½ x 6in)

note

To fit a Samsung S5 mobile phone, but you can make it any size. The multiple is any number of sts (+ 1 for the base ch) (see page 18).

abbreviations

approx. approximate(ly)
ch chain
dc double crochet
rep repeat
RS right side
ss slip stitch
st(s) stitch(es)
tr treble

• •

cosy

This is made in one piece.
Make 1 row stripes using A, B, C, D, E, F, G, H, changing colour on each row.
Row 1: Using any colour make 21ch, 1dc in second ch from hook and each ch to end. (20 sts)
Cut yarn, do not fasten off.
Row 2: Join next colour, 1ch, 1dc in each st to end. (20 sts)
Cut yarn, do not fasten off.
Repeat Row 2 until 72 rows have been worked or to required length.
Fasten off.
Sew in ends.

bow

(make one)
Using D, make 16ch, join with a ss to form a ring.
Round 1 (RS): 1ch (does not count as a st), 1dc in each ch to end, join with a ss in first dc. (16 sts)
Round 2: 3ch, (counts as tr), 1tr in each st to end; join with a ss in top of first 3-ch. (16 sts)
Round 3: 1ch, 1dc in each st to end, join with a ss in first dc.
Fasten off leaving a tail of approx. 45cm (17½in).

finishing

With RS together fold Cosy in half lengthways and sew up side seams.
Block and press.

Turn Bow RS out and hold flat with fasten off st and tail at the top at the front centre. Using yarn tail, wrap yarn around centre of ring tightly to create bow shape, then secure in place on one side of cosy approx. 6 rows from the top, using a yarn sewing needle.

chapter two

cosy living

bunny egg cosies

These cute little egg cosies have bunny ears and are made using standard double crochet to fit an average-sized egg. They are made in a spiral so it's useful to use a stitch marker to mark the beginning and end of each round.

materials

Debbie Bliss Rialto DK, 100% merino wool DK weight yarn
1 x 50g (1¾oz) ball – approx. 105m (115yd) – each of:

A: 58 Grass (green)
B: 44 Aqua (blue)
C: 64 Mauve (pink)
D: 69 Citrus (yellow)

3.5mm (US size E/4) crochet hook

Stitch marker

6 small pink beaded fabric bows

tension

17 sts x 19 rows over a 10cm (4in) square, working double crochet using 3.5mm (US size E/4) hook.

finished measurement

Approx. 4cm (1½in) diameter

abbreviations

approx. approximate(ly)
ch chain
cont continu(e)(ing)
dc double crochet
dc2tog double crochet 2 stitches together
rep repeat
RS right side
st(s) stitch(es)
ss slip stitch
WS wrong side

. . . .

cosy

(make 1 each in A, B, C, and D)
Make 2ch, 6dc into second ch from hook.
Round 1 (RS): 2dc in each dc to end. (12 dc)
Cont in rounds with RS always facing.
Round 2: Rep Round 1. (24 dc)
Rounds 3–7: 1dc in each dc to end.
Round 8: *1dc in next dc, dc2tog over next 2 dc; rep from * to end. (16 dc)
Round 9: 1dc in each dc, join with a ss in first dc of round.
Fasten off.

ears

(make 2 per Cosy)
Row 1: Using A, B, C, or D, make 5ch, 1dc in second ch from hook, 1dc in each ch to end. (4 sts)
Rows 2–5: 1ch, 1dc in each st to end. (4 sts)
Row 6: 1ch, [dc2tog] twice. (2 sts)
Row 7: 1ch, 1dc in each st.
Row 8: 1ch, dc2tog.
Fasten off.

finishing

Sew in ends on WS and turn Cosy RS out.
Pin and block Ears.
Position and pin Ears onto top of RS of Cosy and sew in place.
Sew one bow onto the left-hand Ear.

Row 2: Miss ss from previous row and join MC in last dc made. 1ch, 5tr in same st, miss 2 sts, 1dc in next st (top of shell), 5tr in next st (dc from previous row), miss 2 sts, 1dc in next st (top of shell), miss 2 sts, 5tr in first dc from Row 1.

Row 3: 1ch, 1dc in first st, miss 1 st, 1dc in next st, miss 2 ch, 5tr in next st (dc from previous row), miss 2 sts, 1dc in next st (top of shell), miss 2 sts, 5tr in next st (dc from previous Row), miss 2 sts, 1dc in next st, miss 1 st, 1dc in last st.

Row 4: 1ch, 1dc in first st, 5tr in next st, miss 2 sts, 1dc in next st, miss 2 sts, 5tr in next st, miss 2 sts, 1dc in next st, miss 2 sts, 5tr in next st, 1dc in last st.

Row 5: 1ch, 5tr in first st, miss 2 sts, 1dc in next st, miss 2 sts, 5tr in next st, miss 2 sts, 1dc in next st, miss 2 sts, 5tr in next st, miss 2 sts, 1dc in next st, miss 1 st, 5tr in last st.

Row 6: 1ch, 3tr in first st, miss 1 st, 1dc in next st, miss 2 sts, 5tr in next st, miss 2 sts, 1dc in next st, miss 2 sts, 5tr in next st, miss 2 sts, 1dc in next st, miss 2 sts, 5tr in next st, miss 2 sts, 1dc in next st, miss 1 st, 3tr in last st.

Row 7: 1ch, 3tr, miss 2 sts, 1dc in next st (top of Shell), miss 2 sts, 5tr in next st (dc from previous row), miss 2 sts, 1dc in next st (top of Shell), miss 2 sts, 5tr in next st, miss 2 sts, 1dc in next st, miss 2 sts, 5tr in next st, miss 2 sts, 1dc in next st, miss 2 sts, 3tr in last st.
Cut yarn, do not fasten off.

Row 8: Using A, 1ch, 1dc in each st to end.
Fasten off.

front bottom

Work as for Back for 16 Rows (ending on a Row 2).
Cut yarn, do not fasten off. Join A.

edging:
Rows 1–4: 1ch, 1dc in first st, 1dc in each st to end. (37 sts)
Fasten off.

front top

Using A, make 38ch.

edging:
Row 1: 1dc in second ch from hook, 1dc in each st to end. (37 sts)
Cut yarn, do not fasten off. Join MC.

main pattern:
Row 2: 1ch, 1dc in first st, *miss 2 sts, 5tr in next st, miss 2 sts, 1dc in next st; rep from * to end, ending 1dc in last st.

Row 3: 1ch, 3tr in first st, *miss 2 sts, 1dc in next st (top of Shell), miss 2 sts, 5tr in next st (dc from previous row); rep from * to end, ending with 3tr in last st.
Rep Rows 2–3 until 11 rows of pattern have been made, or approx. 12cm (4¾in), ending on a Row 3.

funnel opening:
Rep Rows 1–7 of Funnel Opening of Back.
Fasten off.

flowers

(make 3, using B, C and D for the flowers and C, B and A for the centres)
Using first colour, make 4ch, join with a ss in first ch to form a ring.
Round 1 (RS): 1ch, 6dc in ring, break off first colour, join second colour with a ss in first dc.
Round 2: Using second colour, *[4ch, 1dtr, 4ch, 1ss] in same st, ss in next st; rep from * five times more (6 petals), working last ss in dc at base of first 4-ch.
Fasten off.

finishing

Sew in ends.
With RS facing upward, place Back of cosy on a flat surface. With RS together place Front Top on top of Back, aligning funnel shape. With RS together and aligning bottom edges, place Front Bottom onto Back – top edge of Front Bottom will overlap bottom edge of Front Top. Pin Front and Back pieces together along sides and bottom only, leaving funnel opening and overlapping dc edges open. Sew pinned seams, then turn cosy RS out.

Using A, join yarn with a ss in any two loops at back of WS of a Flower near centre of Round 1.
Make between 4ch and 6ch for stalk (to make a variation on length), then with RS of cosy facing, join Flower with a ss in any two loops to centre of top at base of Front Top.
Fasten off and sew in ends.
Attach all Flowers in the same way.

Fit onto hot water bottle.

jam jar tea light cosies

These are perfect over little jam jars. They are made using a fine lace yarn and a lace stitch, so that when the candlelight glows through it creates gorgeous textured patterns.

materials

Debbie Bliss Rialto Lace, 100% extra fine merino laceweight yarn
1 x 50g (1¾oz) ball – approx. 390m (427yd) – each of:
07 Fuchsia (bright pink)
033 Candy (pink)
028 Primrose (yellow)
026 Coral (salmon)
018 Aqua (deep aqua)
035 Acid Yellow (yellow-green)

2.5mm (US size C/2) crochet hook

tension

26 sts x 12 rows over 10cm (4in) square, working treble crochet using 2.5mm (US size C/2) hook and Debbie Bliss Rialto Lace.

finished measurement

To fit a 190ml (6.5fl oz) round jam jar

abbreviations

approx. approximate(ly)
ch chain
CL cluster
dc double crochet
rep repeat
RS right side
sp space
st(s) stitch(es)
ss slip stitch
tr treble
tch turning chain
tr3tog treble 3 stitches together
yrh yarn round hook

special abbreviations

3trCL 3 treble cluster – yrh, insert hook in sp, yrh, pull yarn through work (3 loops on hook). Yrh, pull yarn through 2 loops on hook (2 loops on hook). Yrh, insert hook in same sp, yrh, pull yarn through work (4 loops on hook). Yrh, pull yarn through 2 loops on hook (3 loops on hook). Yrh, insert hook in same sp, yrh, pull yarn through work (5 loops on hook). Yrh, pull yarn through 2 loops on hook (4 loops on hook). Yrh, pull yarn through all 4 loops on hook (1 loop on hook).

4trCL 4-treble together cluster (made over 2 sps) – yrh, insert hook in sp, yrh, pull yarn through work (3 loops on hook). Yrh, pull yarn through first two loops on hook (2 loops on hook). Yrh, insert hook in same sp, yrh pull yarn through work (4 loops on hook). Yrh, pull yarn through first two loops on hook (3 loops on hook). Yrh, insert hook in next sp, yrh, pull yarn though (5 loops on hook). Yrh, pull yarn through first two loops on hook (4 loops on hook). Yrh, insert hook in same sp, yrh, pull yarn through work (6 loops on hook). Yrh, pull yarn through first two loops on hook (5 loops on hook). Yrh, pull yarn through all 5 loops on hook (1 loop on hook).

cosy

(make 1 in each colour)

bottom edging:

Row 1: Make 45ch, 1dc in second ch from hook, 1dc in each ch to end. (44 sts)

Row 2: 1ch, 1dc in each st to end. (44 sts)

Row 3 (increase row): 1ch, *1dc in each of next 8 sts, 2dc in next st; rep from * to last 8 sts, 1dc in each of next 7 sts, 2dc in last st. (49 sts)

main pattern:

Row 1 (RS): 1ch, 1dc in first st, 1dc in next st, *4ch, 4trCL over next 5 sts as follows; leaving last loop of each st on hook work 1tr into each of next 2 sts, miss 1 st, 1tr into each of next 2 sts, yrh and draw through all 5 loops on hook; 4ch, 1dc in next st **, 1ch miss 1 st, 1dc in next st; rep from * ending last rep at **, 1dc in last st.

Row 2: 3ch (counts as 1tr), 1tr in first st, *3ch, 1dc in next 4-ch sp, 1ch, miss CL, 1dc in next 4-ch sp, 3ch, miss 1dc **, 3trCL in next 1ch sp; rep from * ending last rep at **, tr2tog in last dc.

Row 3: 1ch, 1dc in first st, *1dc in next ch sp, 4ch, 4trCL as follows: leaving last loop of each st on hook work 2tr in same ch sp, miss [1dc, 1ch, 1dc], 2tr in next ch sp, yrh and draw through all 5 loops on hook; 4ch, 1dc in same ch sp **, 1ch, rep from * ending last rep at **, 1dc in top of 3-ch from previous row.

Rep Rows 2 and 3 three times more and then rep Row 2 once more.

top edging:

Row 1: 1ch, 3dc in first ch sp, miss 1 dc, 1dc in next 1-ch sp, miss 1 dc, [3dc in next 4-ch sp] twice, miss 1 dc, 1dc in next 1-ch sp, miss 1 dc, *3dc in next ch sp, 3dc in next ch sp, miss 1 dc, 1dc in next 1-ch sp, miss 1 dc; rep from * three times more, 3dc in last ch sp, 1dc in top of tr2tog from previous row, 1dc in top of tch. (44 sts)

Rows 2–5: 1ch, 1dc in each st. (44 sts)

Work more dc rows to top lip of jar if necessary.

Fasten off

finishing

With RS together, join seam.

Turn RS out and fit over jar.

bow egg cosies

These cute little things are to place over your eggs to keep them warm, but you won't want to take them off because they're so gorgeous. They make a great gift for a celebration breakfast.

materials

Debbie Bliss Rialto 4ply, 100% merino wool 4ply weight yarn
1 x 50g (1¾oz) ball – approx. 180m (197yd) per ball – each of:
22 Fuchsia (bright pink)
45 Tangerine (orange)
34 Blush (pale pink)
37 Sea green (aqua blue/green)
39 Amber (yellow)
33 Hyacinth (blue)

3mm (US size D/3) crochet hook

25 Size 6 seed beads in white for each cosy

tension

Approx. 20 sts x 25 rows over 10cm (4in) square, working double crochet using 3mm (US size D/3) hook and Debbie Bliss Rialto 4ply yarn.

finished measurement

Approx. 6cm (1⅜in) diameter

abbreviations

approx. approximate(ly)
ch chain
cont continu(e)(ing)
dc double crochet
dc2tog double crochet 2 stitches together
rep repeat
RS right side
st(s) stitch(es)
ss slip stitch
WS wrong side
yrh yarn round hook

special abbreviation

PB place bead – *On a WS row,* insert hook in next dc, yrh, pull yarn through (2 loops now on hook), slide bead up close to work, yrh, pull yarn through both loops on hook to complete beaded dc.

tip for beaded crochet

Remember to thread all the beads on the yarn before beginning.

Note that the beaded double crochet stitches are worked on WS rows so that the beads are snugly positioned on the RS of the crochet.

colourways

Cosy 1: Blush; Bow: Fuchsia
Cosy 2: Fuchsia; Bow: Blush
Cosy 3: Tangerine; Bow: Fuchsia
Cosy 4: Amber; Bow: Hyacinth
Cosy 5: Sea Green; Bow: Amber
Cosy 6: Hyacinth; Bow: Tangerine

• •

cosy

Thread 24 beads onto yarn.
Make 2ch, 6dc into second ch from hook.
Round 1 (RS): 2dc in each dc to end. (12 dc)
Cont in rounds with RS always facing.
Round 2: Rep Round 1. (24 dc)
Round 3: *1dc in next st, 2dc in next st; rep from
* to end. (36 dc)
Rounds 4–9: 1dc in each dc to end.
Round 10: *1dc in next dc, dc2tog over next
2 dc; rep from * to end, join with a ss in first dc
of round. (24 sts)
Turn work.
Round 11 (WS): PB in each st to end, join with
a ss in first st. (24 beaded sts)
Fasten off.

bow

Make 12ch, join with a ss in first ch to form a
circle.
Round 1: 1dc in each ch to end. (12 sts)
Round 2: 1dc in each st to end. (12 sts)
Ss in first st and fasten off leaving a long tail.

finishing

Sew in ends on WS of Cosy and turn RS out.

On Bow, sew in first end on WS. Turn RS out.
Thread remaining bead onto long tail from
fasten-off end, then thread tail into a yarn sewing
needle. Flatten piece with fasten-off st in centre at
back. Wrap tail around centre to create Bow
shape, then sew to secure end, incorporating
bead threaded onto yarn in centre of wrap.
Sew Bow onto top of Cosy.

vase cosy

A lovely easy project and a great starting point in crocheting in the round for a beginner. You don't have to count the rows as you work – just keep crocheting until you reach the required length.

materials

cosy
Debbie Bliss, Rialto DK, 100% wool DK weight yarn
1 x 50g (1¾oz) ball – approx. 105m (115yd) – each of:
MC: 70 Pool (blue)
61 Plum (lilac)
858 Pink (pink)

edging
Debbie Bliss Rialto DK, 100% merino wool DK weight yarn
1 x 50g (1¾oz) ball – approx. 105m (115yd) – of:
A: 058 Grass (green)

flowers and French knots
Louisa Harding Cassia 75% superwash wool, 25% nylon DK weight yarn
1 x 50g (1¾oz) ball – approx. 132m (144yd) – each of:
B: 103 Chick (yellow)
      115 Lipstick (bright pink)
      104 Powder (pale pink)

3mm (US size D/3) crochet hook

4mm (US size G/6) crochet hook

Stitch marker

tension

19 sts x 20 rows over 10cm (4in) square, working double crochet using 4mm (US size G/6) hook and Debbie Bliss, Rialto DK.

finished measurement

To fit a vase approx. 10cm (4in) diameter x 15cm (6in) high

note

The multiple for the edging is 6 sts (see page 18).

abbreviations

approx. approximate(ly)
ch chain
dc double crochet
MC main colour
rep repeat
RS right side
st(s) stitch(es)
ss slip stitch
WS wrong side

- -

cosy

(any multiple of stitches)
Foundation chain: Using 4mm (US size G/6) crochet hook and MC, make 52ch. Join Foundation chain with a ss.
Insert stitch marker.
Round 1: 1dc in same place as ss, 1dc in each ch to end. (52 sts)
Round 2: 1dc in first and each dc to end. (52 sts)
Rep Round 2 until work measures height of vase or 14.5cm (5¾in).
Next row (decrease): *1dc in each of next 11 sts, dc2tog; rep from * to end. (48 sts)
Fasten off.

edging:

Working on WS of work and using 4mm (US size G/6) crochet hook, join A with a ss in any stitch on top edge. *5ch, ss in same st, 7ch, ss in next st, 5ch, ss in same st, 1dc in each of next 4 sts; rep from * to end. Join with a ss in first dc.
Fasten off.

flowers

(make 1 in each colour)
Using 3mm (US size D/3) crochet hook and B, 4ch, join ring with a ss in first ch. 1dc in ring, 5ch, ss in same dc, *1dc in ring, 5ch, ss in same dc; rep from * four more times, ss in first dc to join.
Fasten off.

finishing

Sew in ends on Cosy, and turn RS out.

Sew in ends on Flower. Make a French knot in the centre of each in a contrasting colour. Sew Flowers onto RS in centre of Cosy.

Fit Cosy onto vase with RS facing outward.

tip for crocheting in a circle

Make sure that the chain is not twisted when you join the foundation chain circle, and count carefully in the first round to make sure you have the correct number of stitches (52).

chunky cafetière cosy

A very basic double crochet stitch and superchunky yarn are used to make this great cafetière cosy – it's very quick to make and perfect for keeping coffee warm.

materials

Debbie Bliss Lara, 58% wool, 42% alpaca chunky yarn
1 x 100g (3½oz) ball - approx. 60m (65yd) - of:
MC: 01 Pasha (off white)

Debbie Bliss Baby Cashmerino, 55% wool/33% acrylic/12% cashmere lightweight DK (sport weight) yarn
1 x 50g (1¾oz) ball - approx. 125m (137yd) - of:
A: 92 Orange (orange)

8mm (US size L/11) crochet hook

2 leather buttons

tension

7 sts x 8 rows over a 10cm (4in) square, working double crochet using size 8mm (US size L/11) hook and Debbie Bliss Lara yarn.

finished measurement

17.5 x 17.5cm (7 x 7in), to fit a medium-size 4–6 cup cafetière approx. 30cm (12in) circumference

note

The multiple is any number of sts (+ 1 for the base ch) (see page 18).

abbreviations

approx. approximate(ly)
ch chain
dc double crochet
MC main colour
rep repeat
RS right side
st(s) stitch(es)

cosy

Row 1 (RS): Using MC, make 25ch, 1dc in second ch from hook, 1dc in each ch to end. (24 sts)
Rows 2–13: 1ch, 1dc in each st to end. (24 sts)
If necessary make less or more rows to fit height of cafetière.
Do not fasten off.
Row 14 (button loop): 4ch, 1dc into each st to end.
Fasten off.

finishing

With RS together join top of side seams for approx. 2.5cm (1in), leaving remaining seam open. Turn RS out.
Sew first button to correspond with button loop. Sew second button approx. 1cm (⅜in) from edge on same side as first button. Use holes between stitches as buttonhole for second button.
Make 2 tassels using A, and attach next to each other to RS at top edge.

cold bottle cosy

This is a great cosy for your cold water bottle – it provides shade from the sunlight and makes it easy to spot your bottle on the shelf at the gym. The pattern uses a wave and chevron stitch in stripes.

materials

Debbie Bliss Rialto DK, 100% merino wool DK weight yarn
1 x 50g (1¾oz) ball – approx. 105m (115yd) – each of:
A: 069 Citrus (yellow)
B: 056 Tangerine (orange)
C: 019 Duck Egg (blue)

3.5mm (US size E/4) crochet hook

50cm (20in) ribbon

tension

18 sts x 15 pattern rows over 10cm (4in) square, working Wave and Chevron pattern stitch using 3.5mm (US size E4) hook and Debbie Bliss Rialto DK.

finished measurement

Approx. 22.5 x 16.5cm (9 x 6½in), to fit a 550ml (18.5fl oz) water bottle

note

The multiple is 6 sts + 1 st (+ 1 for the base ch) (see page 18).

abbreviations

approx. approximate(ly)
ch chain
cont continu(e)(ing)
dc double crochet
dc2tog double crochet 2 stitches together
dc3tog double crochet 3 stitches together
dtr double treble
htr half treble
rep repeat
RS right side
sp space
ss slip stitch
st(s) stitch(es)

cosy

Using A, make 37ch, 1dc in second ch from hook, 1dc in each ch to end. (36 sts)
Row 1 (RS): Cont with A, 1ch, miss first st, * 1htr in next st, 1tr in next st, 3dtr in next st, 1tr in next st, 1htr in next st, 1dc in next st; rep from * ending last dc in top of first ch from previous row. Cut yarn, do not fasten off.
Row 2: Join B, 1ch, 1dc in each of next 3 sts, *3dc in next st (centre of 3-dtr from previous row), 1dc in each of next 2 sts, dc3tog over next 3 sts, 1dc in each of next 2 sts; rep from * to last 6 sts, 1dc in each of next 2 sts, 3dc in top of next st (centre of 3-dtr from previous row), 1dc in each of next 2 sts, dc2tog over last st and 1ch from previous row.
Cut yarn, do not fasten off.

Row 3: Join C, 1ch, miss first dc2tog from previous row, 1dc in each of next 3 sts, *3dc in next st, 1dc in each of next 2 sts, dc3tog over next 3 sts, 1dc in each of next 2 sts; rep from * to last 5 sts, 3dc in next st, 1dc in each of next 2 sts, dc2tog over last 2 sts.

Row 4: 4ch, miss first dc2tog from previous row, 1dtr in next st, *1tr in next st, 1htr in next st, 1dc in next st, 1htr in next st, 1tr in next st, dtr3tog over next 3 sts; rep from * ending last rep dtr2tog over last 2 sts.

Row 5: 1ch, miss first st, 1dc in each st to end. (36 sts).

Cut yarn, do not fasten off.

Row 6: Join A, 1ch, miss first st, 1dc in each st to end.

Rows 7–18: Rep Rows 1–6 twice more.

Rows 19–20: Rep Rows 1–2.

Row 21: Using C, rep Row 2.

Row 22: Using A, rep Row 3.

Fasten off.

finishing

Press and then sew in ends. With RS together, join seam. Turn Cosy RS out.

Tie ribbon around centre of bottle to decorate.

embroidered beaded hot water bottle cosy

This pretty and delicate hot water bottle cover is decorated with embroidery stitches and beads.

materials

Louisa Harding Cassia, 75% superwash wool/25% nylon DK weight yarn

50g (1¾oz) balls – approx. 132m (144yd) per ball:
2 balls of MC: 104 Powder (pale pink)
1 ball of A: 115 Lipstick (bright pink)

Scrap of Louisa Harding Cassia 108 Lime (green)

3.5mm (US size E/4) crochet hook

Embroidery thread in variegated citrus (green)

Approx. 113 Size 6 beads in frosted white

Approx. 50 Size 8 beads, AB clear

tension

Approx. 19 sts x 13 rows over 10cm (4in) square working half trebles using 3.5mm (US size E/4) hook and Louisa Harding Cassia yarn.

finished measurement

To fit a hot water bottle 19cm (7½in) wide x 26cm (10½in) long (to shoulder) with a funnel measuring approx. 6cm (2⅜in).

note

The multiple is any number of sts (+ 2 for the base ch) (see page 18).

abbreviations

approx. approximate(ly)
ch chain
dc double crochet
htr half treble
MC main colour
rep repeat
RS right side
st(s) stitch(es)
ss slip stitch
tr treble
WS wrong side

back

Row 1 (RS): Using MC, make 38ch, 1htr in third ch from hook, 1htr in each ch to end. (36 sts)

Row 2: 2ch (does not count as htr), 1htr in each st to end. (36 sts)
Rep Row 2 until work measures approx. 10½in (26cm) or until it reaches base of funnel, ending on a RS Row.

funnel opening:

Row 1: ss in next 12 sts, 1dc in each of next 12 sts, ss in next 12 sts. Fasten off.

Row 2: Turn. Join yarn in first dc from Row 1, working on 12 dc made in Row 1 only, 1ch, 1dc in same st, 1dc in each st to end. (12 sts)

Row 3: 1ch, 1dc in first and each st to end. (12 sts)

Row 4: 1ch, 2dc in first st, 1dc in each st to last st, 2dc in last st. (14 sts)

Row 5: 1ch, 2dc in first st, 1dc in each st to last st, 2dc in last st. (16 sts)

Row 6: Rep Row 4. (18 sts)
Row 7: Rep Row 4. (20 sts)
Row 8: Rep Row 3. (20 sts)
Row 9: Rep Row 4. (22 sts)
Row 10: Rep Row 4. (24 sts)
Cut yarn, do not fasten off.

picot edge:

Next Row (RS): Join A, 1ch, 1dc in same st, 1dc in each of next two sts, *[3ch, ss in first ch], 1dc in each of next 2 sts; rep from * to end, 1dc in last st.
Fasten off.

tip

The Cosy is made in three pieces: the Back, Front Top, and Front Bottom.

front top

Rep as for Back until work measures approx. 14cm (5½in).
funnel opening:
Rep as for Back Funnel Opening.

front bottom

Work as for Back until work measures approx. 14.5cm (5¾in),
finishing on a WS Row.
Cut yarn, do not fasten off.
front bottom edging:
Row 1 (WS): Join A, 1ch, 1dc in first st, 1dc in each st to end.
(36 sts)
Row 2 (RS): 1ch, 1dc in first st, *miss next 2 sts, 5tr in next st, miss
next 2 sts, 1dc in next st; rep from * to end.
Fasten off.
front top edging:
Work on underside of Foundation chain.
Row 1 (WS): With WS facing, join A in first ch, 1ch, 1dc in same
ch, 1dc in each ch to end. (36 sts)
Row 2 (RS): 1ch, 1dc in first st, *miss next 2 sts, 5tr in next st, miss
next 2 sts, 1dc in next st; rep from * to end.
Fasten off.

finishing

Sew in ends.
With RS facing upward, place Back of cosy on a flat surface. With
RS together place Front Top on top of Back, aligning funnel shape.
With RS together and aligning bottom edges, place Front Bottom
onto Back – top edge of Front Bottom will overlap bottom edge of
Front Top.
Pin Front and Back pieces together along sides and bottom only,
leaving funnel opening and overlapping treble shell edges open.
Sew pinned seams, then turn cosy RS out.

Embroider main stems with embroidery thread. Make flower
stems in straight stitch with a French knot at end, using embroidery
thread – see pages 20-21 for how to work embroidery stitches.
Sew clusters of beads to end of each flower stem.

bobble tea cosy

This is a really cute tea cosy – the pattern is a Bobble stitch worked in stripes, with an added touch of bright pink from the pompoms.

materials

Louisa Harding Cassia, 75% superwash wool/25% nylon DK weight yarn

50g (1¾oz) balls - approx. 132m (144yd) per ball:

2 balls of A: 112 Prince (blue)

3 balls of B: 102 Ecru (off white)

1 ball of C: 108 Lime (green)

1 ball of D: 115 Lipstick (pink)

4mm (US size G/6) crochet hook

6mm (US size J/10) crochet hook

tension

Approx. 4 bobbles across (12 sts) x 3 bobble rows (11 rows) over 10cm (4in) square, using 4mm (US size G/6) hook and Louisa Harding Cassia yarn held double.

finished measurement

To fit standard sized 5-cup tea pot

note

The multiple is 3 sts + 1 st (+ 1 for the base ch) (see page 18).

tip

To work with double strands of yarn when only one ball is required for the whole project, wind the ball of yarn into two balls and work with a strand from each small ball placed together.

abbreviations

approx. approximate(ly)

cont continue

dc double crochet

htr half treble

rep repeat

RS right side

ss slip stitch

sts stitch(es)

tch turning chain

tr treble

WS wrong side

yrh yarn round hook

special abbreviation

3trCL 3 treble cluster – yrh, insert hook in st, yrh, pull yarn through work (3 loops on hook). Yrh, pull yarn through 2 loops on hook (2 loops on hook). Yrh, insert hook in same st, yrh, pull yarn through work (4 loops on hook). Yrh, pull yarn through 2 loops on hook (3 loops on hook). Yrh, insert hook in same st, yrh, pull yarn through work (5 loops on hook). Yrh, pull yarn through 2 loops on hook (4 loops on hook). Yrh, pull yarn through all 4 loops on hook (1 loop on hook). Make 1ch to complete 3trCL.

main piece

(make 2, Front and Back)

Working with double strands of yarn throughout.

Row 1 (RS): Using A and 6mm (US size J/10) hook, make 29ch, 1dc in second ch from hook, 1dc in each ch to end. (28 sts)

Row 2: 1dc in each st to end.

Cut yarn, but do not fasten off.

Rows 3–6 are main pattern rows.

Row 3: Join B, 1dc in first st, *3trCL in next st, 1dc in each of next 2 sts; rep from * to end.

Row 4: 1dc in each st to end.

Cut yarn, but do not fasten off.

Rows 5–6: Join A, 1dc in each st to end.

Cut yarn, do not fasten off.

Change to 4mm (US size G/6) hook.

Rows 7–8: Join B, rep Rows 3 and 4.

Cut yarn, do not fasten off.

Rows 9–10: Join A, rep Rows 5 and 6.

Cut yarn, do not fasten off.

Rep Rows 7–10 until work measures approx. 15cm (6in) – or to top of lid – ending on a Row 10.

Do not cut yarn or fasten off.

Use one strand of yarn from this point, changing colours as instructed.

top:

Row 1 (eyelets): Cont using 4mm (US size G/6) hook and A, *1dc in each of next 3 sts, 2ch, miss next 2 sts; rep from * to last 3 sts, 1dc in each of last 3 sts.

Row 2: *1dc in each of next 3 sts, 1dc in top loop of each of next 2 ch; rep from * to last 3 sts, 1dc in each of last 3 sts.

Cut yarn, do not fasten off.

Rows 3–10: Work as main pattern Rows 3–10 above.

Cut yarn, do not fasten off.

top edging:

Join C, 1ch, *1dc in each of next 3 sts, [3ch, 1dc in base of 3-ch] (picot); rep from * ending 1dc in last st.

Fasten off.

Drawstring

Using double strands of C, make a chain measuring approx. 45cm (18in).

Fasten off.

finishing

Sew in ends. With RS of Front and Back together sew side seams using back stitch, leaving gaps for handle and spout. Turn cosy RS out.

Thread Drawstring through eyelets and gather together at top.

Using D, make 2 small pompoms and attach one at each end of Drawstring.

tip

Pin before sewing and try the cosy on your teapot to check you have left a large enough gap for the handle and the spout.

baby cosy

The most perfect cosy – a baby cosy with ears!
This is made in a gorgeous silk mix yarn in a silver
grey, but feel free to use any colour you choose;
it's just important to make sure it's a lovely soft
yarn for the lucky baby.

materials

Fyberspates Scrumptious 4ply, 55% superwash merino, 45% silk
4ply weight yarn
3[3:4] x 100g (3½oz) hanks – approx. 365m (339yd) per
hank – of:
A: 318 Glisten (silver-grey)

Debbie Bliss Rialto 4ply, 100% merino wool 4ply weight yarn
1[1:1] x 50g (1¾oz) ball – approx. 180m (197yd) – of:
B: 39 Amber (yellow)

2.5mm (US size C/2) crochet hook

3mm (US size D/3) crochet hook

tension

33 sts and 18 rows over 10cm (4in) square working patt using
3mm (US size D/3) hook and Fyberspates Scrumptious 4ply.

finished measurement

	Newborn	Baby	Toddler
Width	50	62	77cm
	20	24	30in
Length	60	70	85cm
	23½	27½	33½in

abbreviations

approx. approximate(ly)
ch chain
cont continu(e)(ing)
dc double crochet
dtr double treble
htr half treble
patt pattern
rep repeat
RS right side
st(s) stitch(es)
sp space
ss slip stitch
tch turning chain
tr treble
WS wrong side
yrh yarn round hook

special abbreviations

1htrV-st 1 half treble V-stitch – [1htr, 1ch, 1htr] into next st or sp as directed.

htr2tog yrh, insert hook into next st and draw through loop, rep into next st (5 loops on hook), yrh and draw loop through 5 loops (1 loop on hook).

• •

main piece

Using 2.5mm (US size C/2) hook and A, make 170[197:239]ch.
Foundation row (RS): 1htr into third ch from hook, 1htr in each ch to end.
(169[196:238] sts)
Change to 3mm (US size D/3) hook.
Row 1 (WS): 1ch, 1htr in each of first 2 htr, miss 1 st, *1htrV-st in next st, miss 2 sts; rep from * to end, working last rep as 1htrV-st in next st, miss 1 st, 1htr in next st, 1htr in top of tch of previous row. (55[64:78] patt with 2 htr at each end)

Row 2 (patt row): 1ch, 1htr in each of first 2 htr, miss 1 htr and 1 ch, *1htrV-st in next st, miss next htr and 1-ch; rep from * to end, working last rep as 1htrV-st in next st, 1htr in each of last 2 sts.

Rep last row until work measures approx. 58.5[68.5:83.5]cm (23[27:33]in), ending with RS facing for next row.

left corner shaping:

Next row: 1ch, 1htr in each of first 2 htr, miss 1 htr and 1 ch, *1htrV-st in next st, miss next htr and 1-ch; rep from * to last 5 sts, miss 3 sts, 1htr in each of last 2 sts. (1 patt decrease)

Next row (decrease): 2ch (counts as first htr), 1htr in next st, miss next htr and ch, 1htr in next htr, *miss next htr and 1ch, 1htrV-st in next st; rep from * to end, working last rep as 1htrV-st in next st, miss 1 st, 1htr in next st, 1htr in top of tch. (1 patt decrease, 53[62:76] patts)

Change to 2.5mm (US size C/2) hook.

Next row: 2ch (counts as first htr), 1htr in each st to last 5 sts, [htr2tog over next 2 sts] twice, 2ch, ss in top of tch.

Fasten off.

hood

Using 2.5mm (US size C/2) hook and A, make 129[141:171]ch.

Foundation row (RS): 1htr into third ch from hook, 1htr in each ch to end. (128[140:170] sts)

Change to 3mm (US size D/3) hook.

Row 1 (WS): 1ch, 1htr in first htr, miss 1 st, *1htrV-st in next st, miss 2 sts; rep from * to end, working last rep as 1htrV-st in next st, miss 1 st, 1htr in top of tch.

Next row (decrease): 2ch, miss first 2 htr and 1 ch, 1htr in next htr, *miss 2 sts, 1htrV-st in next st; rep from * to last 4 sts, miss 1 htr and 1 ch, 1htr in next htr. (2 patts decrease, 40[44:54] patts)

Next row: 1ch, 1htr in first htr, *miss 2 sts, 1htrV-st in next st; rep from * to end, 1htr in top of tch.

Rep last 2 rows 5[6:7] times more. (30[32:40] patts)

Next row: Work decrease row as above.

Rep last row until 2 patt remain.

Fasten off.

ears

(make 2 in A for outer ear and 2 in B for inner ear)

Using 2.5mm (US size C/2) hook, make 12ch.

Row 1(RS): 1htr into second ch from hook, 1htr in each of next 9 ch, 3htr in next ch, 1htr into each ch on opposite side of ch, turn. (23 htr)

Row 2 (WS): 2ch (counts as 1 st), miss first st, 1htr in each of next 10 htr, 3htr in next st, 1htr in each of next 10 htr, 1htr in top of tch, turn. (25 sts)

Row 3: 1ch, 1dc in each of first 3 htr, 1htr in each of next 3 htr,
[1tr in next htr, 2tr in next htr] 6 times, 1tr in next htr, 1htr in each of next 3 htr, 1dc in each of next 2 htr, 1dc in top of tch. (31 sts)
Row 4: 1ch, 1dc in each of first 2 sts, 1tr in each of next 3 sts,
[2dtr in next st] 21 times, 1tr in each of next 3 sts, 1dc in each of next 2 sts. (52 sts)
Fasten off.

finishing

Place WS of outer Ear to WS of inner Ear. With inner Ear facing, rejoin A to lower edge of Ear and work 1 round of dc through both layers. Fasten off.

With RS of Hood and RS of Main Piece facing each other, position Hood to left-hand corner of Main Piece, matching shaping, and pin in place. Using 2.5mm (US size C/2) hook and A, join outer edge using one row of dc. Fasten off.
Fold Hood back so that WS faces WS of Main Piece.
Sew Ears in place on Hood.

outer edging

Using 3mm (US size D/3) hook, rejoin A to any edge of Body, work one round of dc around edges and across rim of Hood, working 3dc into each corner.
Break yarn, join in B and work 1 round of htr around all outer edges, working 3htr around each corner and working htr2tog where hood joins body. Fasten off.

embroidered jam jar covers

Jars are ideal for keeping crochet hooks, pencils and crochet knick knacks at hand. These are to fit jam jars that are all the same width, but just different heights. If your jam jar is narrower, use fewer stitches and crochet up to the required height. The embroidery is a great way to embellish the cosies using basic stitches and knots.

materials

cosies

Louisa Harding Cassia, 75% superwash wool/25% nylon DK weight yarn
1 x 50g (1¾oz) ball - approx. 132m (144yd) - each of:
A: 115 Lipstick (bright pink)
B: 103 Chick (yellow)
C: 105 Glacier (blue)

3mm (US size D/3) crochet hook

Stitch marker

Embroidery needle

pink holder:
Variegated embroidery thread: citrus (green), claret (reds/purple), damson (purple)

138 Size 10 seed beads in green

yellow holder:
Variegated embroidery thread: citrus (green), claret (reds/purple)

Scraps of green yarn

blue holder:
Variegated embroidery thread: aquarius (blue), citrus (green), carnation (pink)

tension

20 sts x 22 rows over 10cm (4in) square, working double crochet using 3.5mm (US size E/4) hook and Louisa Harding Cassia yarn.

finished measurement

To fit a jam jar of approx. 23cm (9in) circumference, and made to the required height

abbreviations

approx. approximate(ly)
ch chain
dc double crochet
rep repeat
st(s) stitch(es)
ss slip stitch

holder

Foundation chain: Using A, B or C make 44ch. Join Foundation chain with a ss. Insert stitch marker.
Round 1: 1dc in each ch to end. (44 sts)
Round 2: 1dc in each st to end. (44 sts)
Rep Round 2 until work reaches top curve of jar.
Fasten off.

finishing

Sew in ends, turn RS out.

pink holder:
Using embroidery thread, stitch flower petals using bullion knots with French knots in centre. Work Feather stitch for stems and borders (see page 20 for details of embroidery stitches). Sew a bead onto tip of each stem on borders. Fit onto jam jar.

yellow holder:
Using embroidery thread and scraps of green yarn, embroider stems and French knots. Embroider flowers using damson embroidery thread, using lazy daisy stitch, buttonhole wheels, straight stitch and feather stitch.

blue holder:
Using embroidery thread, embroider flowers in blue and pink using lazy daisy stitch, straight stitch and French knots. Embroider leaves in green using single chain stitches.

tip
Work the embroidery stitches loosely to keep the crochet fabric stretchy enough to fit the jar but not to slip down it.

mug cosies

These make a very cute present, and they're also great for keeping your own cup of tea or coffee nice and warm.

materials

Debbie Bliss Rialto DK, 100% merino wool DK weight yarn
1 x 50g (1¾oz) ball – approx. 105m (115yd) per ball – for each cosy:
69 Citrus (yellow)
71 Jade (green)

3.5mm (US size E/4) crochet hook

1 button per cosy

tension

17 sts x 19 rows over 10cm (4in) square, working double crochet using 3.5mm (US size E/4) hook and Debbie Bliss Rialto DK.

finished measurement

26 x 7.5cm (10¼ x 3in), to fit an average sized mug

note

The multiple is 14 sts + 1 st (+ 1 for the base ch) (see page 18).

abbreviations

approx. approximate(ly)
ch chain
dc double crochet
rep repeat
RS right side
ss slip stitch
st(s) stitch(es)
tr treble

cosy

Row 1: Make 16ch, 1dc in second ch from hook, 1dc in each ch to end. (15 sts)
Row 2 (RS): 3ch, 3tr in first st, *miss 3 sts, 1dc in each of next 7 sts, miss 3 sts, 4tr in last st.
Row 3: 1ch, 1dc in each st to end, 1dc in top of 3-ch from previous row. (15 sts)
Row 4: 1ch, 1dc in each of first 4 sts, miss 3 sts, 7tr in next st, miss 3 sts, 1dc in last 4 sts.
Row 5: 1ch, 1dc in each st to end. (15 sts)
Row 6: 3ch, 3tr in first st, miss 3 sts, 1dc in each of next 7 sts, miss 3 sts, 4tr in last st.
Rep Rows 2–6 five more times.
Rep Rows 2–5 once more.

tab:

Row 1: Ss in each of next 4 sts, 1dc in each of next 7 sts, ss in each of next 4 sts.
Fasten off.
Row 2: With RS facing, rejoin yarn in first dc from previous Row. 1ch, 1dc in same st, 1dc in each of next 6 sts, turn. (7 sts)
Row 3: 1ch, 1dc in first st, 1dc in each of next 6 sts. (7 sts)
Row 4: Rep Row 3.
Row 5 (buttonhole): 1ch, 1dc in each of next 2 sts, miss 3 ch, 1dc in last 2 sts.
Row 6: 1ch, 1dc in each of next 2 sts, 3dc in ch sp, 1dc in each of last 2 sts.
Fasten off.

finishing

Sew in ends.
Sew on button on other side of Cosy to align with buttonhole.

bobble cafetière cosy

The bobble stitch used for this cosy creates a lovely thick fabric, which will keep your coffee piping hot.

materials

Debbie Bliss Blue Faced Leicester DK, 100% wool DK weight yarn
1 x 50g (1¾oz) ball – approx. 108m (118yd) – each of:

A: 08 Rose (pale pink)
B: 15 Sage (dark green)
C: 17 Amber (yellow)
D: 13 Pale Blue (blue)
E: 09 Fuchsia (dark pink)
F: 16 Willow (pale green)
G: 11 Heather (purple)

4mm (US size G/6) crochet hook

1 large wooden button

2 small wooden buttons

tension

Approx. 4 bobbles across x 10 bobble rows over 10cm (4in) square, using 4mm (US size G/6) hook and Debbie Bliss Blue Faced Leicester DK yarn.

finished measurement

Approx. 30 x 17.5cm (12 x 7in), to fit a medium-size 4–6 cup cafetière, approx. 30cm (12in) circumference

note

The multiple is 4 sts + 3 sts (+ 1 for the base ch) (see page 18).

abbreviations

approx. approximate(ly)
ch chain
cont continu(e)(ing)
dc double crochet
dc2tog double crochet 2 stitches together
rep repeat
RS right side
st(s) stitch(es)
ss slip stitch
tr treble
WS wrong side

special abbreviation

5trCL 5 treble cluster/bobble – yrh, insert hook in st, yrh, pull yarn through work (3 loops on hook). Yrh, pull yarn through first 2 loops on hook (2 loops on hook). Yrh, insert hook in same st, yrh, pull yarn through work (4 loops on hook), yrh, pull yarn through first 2 loops on hook (3 loops left on hook). Yrh, insert hook in same st, yrh, pull yarn through work (5 loops on hook), yrh, pull yarn through first 2 loops on hook (4 loops left on hook). Yrh, insert hook in same st, yrh, pull yarn through work (6 loops on hook), yrh, pull yarn through first 2 loops on hook (5 loops left on hook). Yrh, insert hook in same st, yrh, pull yarn through work (7 loops on hook), yrh, pull yarn through first 2 loops on hook (6 loops left on hook). Yrh, pull yarn through all 6 loops on hook (1 loop left on hook). Make 1ch to complete 5trCL.

cosy

Work from top to bottom of Cosy.

Using A, make 44ch.

Row 1 (RS): 1dc in second ch from hook, 1dc in each ch to end. (43 sts)

begin bobble pattern:

Row 2 (WS): 1ch, *1dc in each of next 3 sts, 5trCL in next st; rep from * to last 3 sts, 1dc in each of last 3 sts. (10 bobbles).
Cut yarn, do not fasten off.

Row 3: Join B, 1ch, *1dc in each of next 3 sts, 1dc in top of next 5trCL; rep from * to last 3 sts, 1dc in each of last 3 sts.

Row 4: 1ch, 1dc in first st, 5trCL in next st, *1dc in each of next 3 sts, 5trCL in next st; rep from * to last st, 1dc in last st. (11 bobbles)
Cut yarn, do not fasten off.

Row 5: Join C, 1ch, 1dc in first st, *1dc in top of next 5trCL, 1dc in each of next 3 sts; rep from * to last 5trCL, 1dc in top of last 5trCL, 1dc in last st.

Rep Rows 2–5, using A, B, C, D, E, F and G to change colour every two Rows until 16 bobble rows have been worked ending on a Row 5.
Fasten off.

edging:

With RS facing, join A in top left-hand corner (of Row 1).

Row 1:
Side 1
1ch, [1dc in each of next 5 rows down first side edge, dc2tog over next 2 rows] 4 times, 1dc in each row to corner (second corner), [1dc, 1ch, 1dc] in corner st.
Bottom edge
*1dc in top of 5trCL, 1dc in each of next 3 sts; rep from * to next corner. [1dc, 1ch, 1dc] in corner st.
Side 2
[1dc in each of next 5 rows down first side edge, dc2tog over next 2 rows] 4 times, 1dc in each row to corner (third corner), [1dc, 1ch, 1dc] in corner st.
Top edge
*1dc in each of next 3 sts, 1dc in top of 5trCL; rep from * to next corner, [1dc, 1ch, 1dc] in corner st, join with a ss in first dc.

Row 2: 1ch, work a dc edge by working 1dc in each st and 3dc in each corner ch sp, join with a ss in first dc.
Fasten off.

tab

Using A, make 13ch.

Row 1: 1dc in 8th ch from hook, 1dc in each of next 5 ch.

Row 2: 1ch, 1dc in each of next 6 dc, 1dc in each of next 3 ch, 2dc in next ch, 1dc in each of next 9 ch (working on underside of these 9 ch).

Row 3: 1ch, 1dc in each of next 9 dc, 2dc in each of next 2 dc, 1dc in each of next 8 dc, ss in last dc.
Fasten off.

finishing

With RS together join top of side seams for approx. 2.5cm (1in) leaving remaining seam open.

Turn RS out.

With RS together, sew Tab to bottom of side edge, approx. 1cm (⅜in) from corner.

Sew large button on bottom of Cosy to correspond with buttonhole on Tab.

Sew small buttons on edging: Button 1 between second and third bobble from bottom and Button 2 between second and third bobble from top, on same side as large button.

small button loops

With RS facing, and using A, join yarn to align with side of Button 1, in dc of edging on same side as Tab. 1ch, 1dc in same st, 3ch, miss 1 st, 1dc in next st. Fasten off.

Repeat for Button 2. Fasten off.

Sew in ends.

tip
When working a double crochet into the top of the 5-treble cluster, make the double crochet stitch into the chain at the top of the cluster.

daisy tea cosy

A very pretty summertime tea cosy for sipping tea in the garden. The cosy is made in an Aran weight using the yarn doubled, and the flowers are made using a delicate 4ply yarn.

materials

main cosy

Debbie Bliss Blue Faced Leicester Aran, 100% wool aran weight yarn

2 x 50g (1¾oz) balls – approx. 150m (164yd) – of:
MC: 15 Mint (light green)

daisies

Debbie Bliss Rialto 4ply, 100% merino wool 4ply weight yarn

1 x 50g (1¾oz) ball – approx. 180m (197yd) – each of:
A: 39 Amber (yellow)
B: 01 White (white)

6mm (US size J/10) crochet hook

3mm (US size D/3) crochet hook

tension

11 sts x 13 rows over a 10cm (4in) square working double crochet, using 6mm (US size J/10) hook and Debbie Bliss Blue Faced Leicester Aran yarn doubled (2 strands).

finished measurement

To fit a medium-size 2-pint teapot (4–6 cups).

Approx. 17.5cm (7in) from top to bottom, 20cm (8in) wide from centre of handle to edge of spout

abbreviations

approx. approximate(ly)
ch chain
cont continu(e)(ing)
dc double crochet
dc2tog double crochet 2 stitches together
MC main colour
rep repeat
RS right side
ss slip stitch
st(s) stitch(es)
WS wrong side
yrh yarn round hook

note

Use MC yarn doubled throughout by winding main ball into two smaller balls and using 2 strands together.

main piece

(make 2, Front and Back)
Using MC double and 6mm (US size J/10) hook, make 27ch.
Row 1 (RS): 1dc in second ch from hook, 1dc in each ch to end. (26 sts)
Rows 2–4: 1ch, 1dc in each st to end. (26 sts)
Row 5: 1ch, dc2tog, 1dc in each st to last 2 sts, dc2tog. (24 sts)
Rep Row 2 until work measures 10cm (4in). (24 sts)
Next row: 1ch, dc2tog, 1dc in each st to last 2 sts, dc2tog. (22 sts)
Rep the last row until 8 sts remain.
Next row: 1ch, [dc2tog] 4 times. (4 sts)
Next row: 1ch, 1dc in each st to end. (4 sts)
Fasten off.

tab

Using MC double and 6mm (US size J/10) hook, make 4ch.
Row 1: 1dc in second ch from hook, 1dc in each ch to end. (3 sts)
Row 2: 1ch, 1dc in each st to end. (3 sts)
Rep Row 2 thirteen times more.
Fasten off.

daisies

(make approx. 75)
Using A and 3mm (US size D/3) hook, make 4ch, ss in first ch to make a ring.
Round 1: 1ch, 9dc in ring, join with a ss in first dc.
Cut yarn but do not fasten off.
Round 2: Join B, 7ch, ss in same dc (first petal), *ss in next dc, 7ch, ss in same dc; rep from * to end. (9 petals)
Fasten off.
Sew in ends of yellow, leave one strand from white for sewing onto cosy.

finishing

With RS together, pin Front and Back of cosy with long plastic-headed pins, then slip it over your tea pot and take the pins out where the handle and spout go. I use contrasting coloured yarn as stitch markers to mark these spaces. Remove the cosy from the tea pot.

Take the pin out of the top of the cosy. Fold the Tab in half. Put folded end into the top of the tea cosy and insert all the way down leaving the 2 unfolded edges in line with the top edge of the tea cosy, so you can just see them poking through. Pin this in place.

Sew up sides and top of Cosy, incorporating the Tab at the top and leaving the gaps open between the stitch markers for the handle and spout. Sew in ends, turn RS out. You'll see that the Tab is now in place with the loop sticking out at the top.

Sew Daisies onto both sides of Cosy and 1 on each side of Tab.

chapter three

cosy & tidy

passport holder

Easy to find in your handbag, protects your passport and totally individual! This is a lovely V-stitch pattern and ideal as a beginner's project.

materials

Louisa Harding Cassia 75% superwash wool, 25% nylon DK weight yarn

1 x 50g (1¾oz) ball – approx. 132m (144yd) – each of:
A: 112 Prince (blue)
B: 101 White (white)

3mm (US size D/3) crochet hook

Approx. 25cm (10in) square of lining fabric

½m (½yd) of red ribbon

tension

Approx. 9 htrV-sts sts x 15 pattern rows over 10cm (4in) square, using 3mm (US size D/3) hook and Louisa Harding Cassia yarn.

finished measurement

Approx. 15 x 11.5cm (6 x 4½in)

abbreviations

approx. approximate(ly)
ch chain
dc double crochet
htr half treble
rep repeat
st(s) stitch(es)
ss slip stitch
tch turning chain
WS wrong side

special abbreviations

1htrV-st 1 half treble V-stitch – [1htr, 1ch, 1htr] into next st or sp as directed.

1dcV-st 1 double crochet V-stitch – [1dc, 1ch, 1dc] into next st or sp as directed.

main piece

(make 2, Front and Back)
Work in multiples of 2 + 1.
Using A, make 21ch. 1dc in second ch from hook, 1dc in each ch to end. (20 sts)
Row 1(RS): Using A, 2ch (tch), *miss next st, 1htrV-st in next st; rep from * to last 2 sts, miss next st, 1htr in last st.
Row 2: Using A, 2ch (tch), *1htrV-st in next ch sp (between previous V-sts); rep from * to end, 1htr in top of tch. Break yarn, do not fasten off.
Row 3: Using B, 1ch (tch), *1dcV-st in next ch sp (between previous V-sts); rep from * to end, 1dc in 2-ch. Break yarn, do not fasten off.
Rows 4–6: Using A, 2ch (tch), *1htrV-st in next ch sp (between previous V-sts); rep from * to end, 1htr in top of tch.
After Row 6, break yarn, do not fasten off.
Row 7: Rep Row 3.
Rep Rows 4–7 until work measures approx. 15cm (6in).
Fasten off.

finishing

Block piece if necessary and sew in ends.
With RS together, join side and bottom seams.

Make and insert lining and ribbon for ties at top edge, following instructions on page 22, Method 1.

paperback cosy

Protect your books with this pretty book cosy. It makes a great gift for a bookworm, protects paperbacks and is made using a simple double crochet stitch in stripes.

materials

Debbie Bliss Blue Faced Leicester DK, 100% wool DK weight yarn
1 x 50g (1¾oz) ball – approx. 108m (118yd) – each of:
A: 08 Rose (pink)
B: 17 Amber (yellow)
C: 09 Fuchsia (bright pink)
D: 11 Heather (purple)
E: 16 Willow (green)
F: 13 Pale blue (blue)

3.5mm (US size E/4) crochet hook

tension

19 sts x 21 rows over 10cm (4in) square, working double crochet using 3.5mm (US size E/4) hook and Debbie Bliss Blue Faced Leicester DK yarn.

finished measurement

Approx. 14 x 20.5cm (5½ x 8¼in)

note

The multiple is any number of sts (+ 1 for the base ch) (see page 18).

The multiple is any number of sts (+ 1 for the base ch) (see page 18).

abbreviations

approx. approximate(ly)
ch chain
cont continu(e)(ing)
dc double crochet
RS right side
st(s) stitch(es)
WS wrong side

· ·

main piece

Row 1 (RS): Using A, make 26ch, 1dc in second ch from hook, 1dc in each ch to end. (25 sts)
Rows 2–5: Cont with same colour, 1dc in each st to end. (25 sts) Break yarn, do not fasten off.
Each following row: Make 1ch, 1dc in each st to end, breaking yarn when colour change is necessary and not fastening off.
Use colours as follows:
Two rows B.
One row C.
Two rows B.
Six rows D.
Two rows E.
One row C.
Two rows E.
Six rows F.
Two rows A.
One row C.
Two rows A.
Twenty rows E.
Two rows A.
One row C.
Two rows A.
Six rows F.
Two rows E.
One row C.
Two rows E.

Six rows D.
Two rows B.
One row C.
Two rows B.
Row 80-85: A
Fasten off.

top edging:
Join D on RS in first st of one short end.

Row 1: 1ch, 1dc in first st, 1dc in each st to end. (25 sts)

Row 2-3: 1ch, 1dc in each st to end.
Fasten off.
Repeat edging on other short end.

spines

(make 2)

These Spines are made to fit a book cover 19.5 x 13 x 2cm
(7¾ x 5 x ¾in). They should be approx. the same length as the Main Piece when it has been folded in half, allowing approx. 6 rows at the bottom for the width of the book.

Row 1: Using F, make 38ch, 1dc in second ch from hook, 1dc in each ch to end. (37 sts)

Rows 2-5: 1ch, 1dc in each st to end.
Fasten off.
Pin and block.

finishing

Sew in ends. Pin and block.

Fold Main Piece with WS together (RS facing). Place marker at centre fold at bottom on side edge. Place marker in centre of one short edge of Spine. Pin Spine lengthways down one Main Piece side edge only, with WS together and matching markers at bottom. (Remove these markers once side is pinned). Place a marker in each of two corners at bottom of Spine.

Starting at top edge, join B (yellow) with a ss through both pieces. Make a dc seam along first edge by making 34dc evenly down edge to first marker (first corner of Spine), make 2dc in corner, 2dc in along second short edge.

Take out pins along first edge just joined. Pin Spine and Main Piece along second edge. Make 34dc evenly along second edge.
Fasten off.

Repeat on other side.

crochet hook cosy

At home I keep my crochet hooks in jam jars (see page 82 for cosy), but when I go out I like to take a portable crochet hook cosy and this is just the perfect size. It's made in the round, using spirals, and it makes a great gift for someone with a set of crochet hooks inside.

materials

Louisa Harding Cassia, 75% superwash wool/25% nylon DK weight yarn

1 x 50g (1¾oz) ball - approx. 132m (144yd) - each of:

A: 112 Prince (blue)
B: 102 Ecru (off white)

3mm (US size D/3) crochet hook

Stitch marker

1 small button

tension

20 sts x 22 rows over 10cm (4in) square, working double crochet using 3mm (US size D/3) hook and Louisa Harding Cassia yarn.

finished measurement

Approx. 5.5 x 20cm (2¼ x 8in)

abbreviations

approx. approximately
ch chain
cont continu(e)(ing)
dc double crochet
dc2tog double crochet 2 stitches together
MC main colour
st(s) stitch(es)
ss slip stitch

cosy

Using A, make 2ch, 6dc in second ch from hook. Place a stitch marker in loop on hook.

Round 1: 2dc in each st to end. (12 sts)
Round 2: 2dc in each st to end. (24 sts)
Rounds 3–4: 1dc in back loop of each st to end. (24 sts)
Work should now look like a small bowl curving inwards. Turn work out so that ridges formed by working in back loops are on outside. Cont to work on this side of work.
Round 5: Working in both loops of each st, 1dc in each st to end. (24 sts)
Cont working 1dc in each st, in a spiral, until work measures approx. 17cm (6¾in) or until piece is same size as length of crochet hooks.
Turn, then begin working in rows.
Next 12 rows: 1ch, 1dc in each of next 13 sts. (13 sts)
Next row: 1ch, dc2tog, 1dc in each of next 9 sts, dc2tog. (11 sts)
Next row: 1ch, 1dc in each st to end. (11 sts)
Next row: 1ch, dc2tog, 1dc in each of next 7 sts, dc2tog. (9 sts)
Next row: 1ch, 1dc in each st to end. (9 sts)
Next row: 1ch, dc2tog, 1dc in each of next 5 sts, dc2tog. (7 sts)
Next row (buttonhole): 1ch, dc2tog, 2ch, miss next 3 sts, dc2tog.
Next row: 1ch, 2dc in ch sp, ss in last st. (4 sts).
Cut yarn, do not fasten off.
edging:
Join B, 1ch, make approx. 21dc down first side, 1dc in each st along front edge, make approx. 25dc along second side and top to join. Join with a ss in first dc.
Fasten off.

finishing

Sew in ends, then sew on button to match buttonhole.

soap cosies

I travel a lot and I like to take my favourite soap with me. A soap cosy is exactly what I need to wrap it in – and I can use the cosy as a bathroom cloth afterwards, dry it, then stick the soap back in it again for travelling home.

materials

For each cosy
DMC Natura Just Cotton, 100% cotton 4ply yarn
1 x 50g (1¾oz) ball – approx. 155m (169yd) per ball – for each cosy:
A: N30 Glicine (lilac)
B: N06 Rose Layette (pale pink)
C: N87 Glacier (pale blue)
D: N52 Geranium (dark pink)

3mm (US size D/3) crochet hook

1 small button for each cosy

tension

4 Shells across x 12 rows of Shell stitch over 10cm (4in) square, using 3mm (US size D/3) hook and DMC Natura Just Cotton.

finished measurement

15cm (6in) square, to fit a soap bar measuring approx. 7cm (2¾in) square

note

The multiple is 6 sts + 1 sts (+ 1 for the base ch) (see page 18).

abbreviations

approx. approximate(ly)
ch chain
ch sp chain space
dc double crochet
rep repeat
RS right side
st(s) stitch(es)
sp space
ss slip stitch
tch turning chain
tr treble
WS wrong side

special abbreviation

Shell stitch – [2tr, 1ch, 2tr] in same ch or sp.

• •

cosy

Make 38ch.
Row 1 (RS): 1dc in second ch from hook. *miss next 2 ch, Shell in next ch, miss next 2 ch, 1dc in next ch; rep from * to end.
Row 2 (WS): 3ch, 2tr first dc, 1dc in 1-ch sp of next Shell; *Shell in next dc, 1dc in 1-ch sp of next Shell; rep from * to end, ending last rep with 3tr in last dc.
Row 3: 1ch, 1dc in first tr, *Shell in next dc, 1dc in 1-ch sp of next Shell; rep from * to end, working last dc of last rep in top of tch.
Rep Rows 2 and 3 until work measures 15cm (6in) or Cosy is a square.
Do not fasten off.
button loop:
Make 6ch, join with a ss in same st.
Fasten off.

finishing

Sew in ends.
Place soap diagonally in centre of WS of cosy, with button loop at top. Fold side corners over soap, fold bottom corner over top of sides, fold top corner (with button loop) down. Mark where button matches button loop and sew on button in marked place.

sunglasses case

I'm constantly leaving my sunglasses around and getting them scratched. This cosy will protect your shades and is a really fun project to make over the summer.

materials

Louisa Harding Cassia, 75% superwash wool/25% nylon DK weight yarn

1 x 50g (1¾oz) ball – approx. 132m (144yd) – each of:
A: 124 (dark pink)
B: 105 Glacier (pale blue)
C: 104 Powder (pale pink)
D: 107 Lilac (lilac)
E: 112 Prince (mid blue)

3mm (US size D/3) crochet hook

Approx. 56 x 13cm (22 x 5¼in) of cotton lining fabric

tension

7cm (2¾in) square using 3mm (US size D/3) hook and Louisa Harding Cassia yarn.

finished measurement

Approx. 25 x 10cm (10 x 4in)

abbreviations

approx. approximate(ly)
ch chain
ch sp chain space
dc double crochet
rep repeat
RS right side
ss slip stitch
st(s) stitch(es)
tr treble

special abbreviation

2trCL 2 treble cluster – yrh, insert hook in st or sp, yrh, pull yarn through work (3 loops on hook). Yrh, pull yarn through 2 loops on hook (2 loops on hook). Yrh, insert hook in same st or sp, yrh, pull yarn through work (4 loops on hook). Yrh, pull yarn through 2 loops on hook (3 loops on hook). Yrh, pull yarn through all 3 loops on hook (1 loop on hook).

colourway

Use either A, B, C, D for Rounds 1, 2, 3 and always use E for Round 4.

squares

(make 9)
Using A, make 6ch, join with a ss in first ch to form a ring.
Round 1 (RS): 4ch, [1tr, 1ch in ring] 11 times, join with a ss in third of first 4-ch.
Cut yarn, do not fasten off.
Round 2: Join B in next 1-ch sp, 3ch, 1tr in same ch sp, [3ch, 2trCL in next ch sp] 11 times, 3ch, join with a ss in top of first 3-ch. (12 x 2trCL)
Cut yarn, do not fasten off.
Round 3: Join C in top of next 2trCL, 1ch, 1dc in same st, 1ch, miss first 3-ch sp and 2trCL, *[3tr, 3ch, 3tr in next ch sp] (corner), 1ch, miss next 2trCL and next 3-ch sp, 1dc in top of next 2trCL, 1ch, miss next 3-ch sp and next 2trCL; rep from * three times more, ending last rep with a ss in top of first dc.
Cut yarn, do not fasten off.
Round 4: Join D in same dc, 1ch, 1dc in same st, 1dc in first ch sp, *1dc in each of next 3 sts, 3dc in corner ch sp, 1dc in each of next 3 sts, 1dc in next ch sp, 1dc in next dc, 1dc in next ch sp; rep from * three times more, 1dc in each of next 3 sts, 3dc in corner ch sp, 1dc in each of next 3 sts, 1dc in next ch sp, join with a ss in first dc.
Fasten off.

finishing

Block and press Squares lightly.
Place Squares on a flat surface and arrange following the diagram (see opposite). Sew Squares together into the shaped piece.

Sew lining (see page 22, Method 2).

Fold piece into glasses cosy shape along dotted lines, matching letters. Pin and sew with RS together. Turn RS out.
Block and press again.

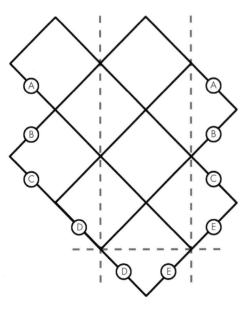

glasses cosy

I love the soft feel of this cosy, which is made using a delicious blend of hand-dyed silk and merino. This case is big enough to hold an average-sized pair of glasses.

materials

Fyberspates Scrumptious 4ply, 55% superwash merino wool, 45% silk 4ply yarn
1 x 3½oz (100g) hank – approx. 365m (399yd) – of 318 Glisten (silver-grey)

3mm (US size D/3) crochet hook

5 Size 6 white seed beads

Small snap fastener

30 x 20cm (12 x 8in) of cotton lining fabric

tension

4 Shells x 13 Shell st rows over a 10cm (4in) square using a 3mm (US size D/3) hook and Fyberspates Scrumptious DK yarn.

finished measurement

Approx. 14.5cm (5¾in) wide x 8.5cm (3½in) long (when folded with flap down)

note

The multiple is 6 sts + 1 sts (+ 1 for the base ch) (see page 18).

abbreviations

approx. approximate(ly)
ch chain
dc double crochet
dc2tog double crochet 2 stitches together
htr half treble
rep repeat
RS right side
ss slip stitch
st(s) stitch(es)
tr treble
tr2tog treble 2 stitches together
WS wrong side

special abbreviations

5tr-Shell – make 5tr in same stitch.

3tr-Shell – make 3tr in same stitch.

cosy

Make 38ch.
Row 1 (RS): 1dc in second ch from hook, 1dc in each ch to end. (37 sts)
Row 2: 1ch, 1dc in first st, *miss next 2 sts, 5tr in next st (5tr-Shell), miss next 2 sts, 1dc in next st; rep from * to end of row.
Row 3: 3ch, 2tr in first st, *miss next 2 sts, 1dc in next st (centre st of Shell), miss next 2 sts, 5tr in next dc; rep from * to end, ending last rep with 3tr in last dc.
Row 4: 1ch, 1dc in first st, *miss next 2 sts, 5tr in next dc (5tr-Shell), miss next 2 sts, 1dc in next st (centre st of Shell); rep from * ending last rep with 1dc in top of first 3-ch from previous row.
Row 5: Rep Row 3.
Rep Rows 4–5 until work measures approx. 18cm (7¼in) ending on a Row 4.

flap:

Row 1: 3ch, 2tr in first dc, *miss next 2 sts, 1dc in next st, miss next 2 sts, 5tr in next dc; rep from * ending 3tr in last dc. (5 x 5tr-Shells)
Row 2: 1ch, miss first st, 1dc in next st (centre st of 3tr-Shell), miss 1 st, 3tr in next dc, *miss 2 sts, 1dc in next st, miss 2 sts, 5tr in next dc; rep from * to end, ending 3tr in last dc, miss 2 sts, 1dc in top of 3-ch from previous row. (5 x 5tr-Shells)

Row 3: 2ch, miss first 2 sts, 1dc in next st (centre of 3tr-Shell), miss next st, 3tr in next st, *miss 2 sts, 1dc in next st, miss next 2 sts, 5tr in next st; rep from * twice more, miss 2 sts, 1dc in next st, miss 2 sts, 3tr in next dc, miss next st, 1dc in next st (centre of 3tr-Shell), miss next st, 1htr in last dc. (3x 5tr-Shells)

Row 4: 2ch, miss first 3 sts, 1dc in next st, miss next st, 3tr in next st, miss next 2 sts, 1dc in next st, *miss next 2 sts, 5tr in next st, miss next 2 sts, 1dc in next st; rep from * once more, miss 2 sts, 3tr in next dc, miss next st, 1dc in next st (centre of 3tr-Shell), miss next st, 1htr in last dc. (2 x 5tr-Shells)

Row 5: 2ch, miss first 3 sts, 1dc in next st (centre of 3tr-Shell), miss next st, 5tr in next st, *miss next 2 sts, 1dc in next st, miss next 2 sts, 5tr in next st; rep from * once more, miss next st, 1dc in next st (centre of 3tr-Shell), miss next 2 sts, 1htr in top of first 2-ch from previous row. (3 x 5tr-Shells)

Row 6: 3ch, miss first 4 sts, 1dc in next st, *miss next 2 sts, 5tr in next st, miss next 2 sts, 1dc in next st; rep from * once more, miss next 3 sts, 1tr in top of first 2-ch from previous row. (2 x 5tr-Shells)
Fasten off.

flower

Make 4ch, join with a ss to form a ring.
Round 1: [3ch, tr2tog in ring, 3ch, ss in ring] five times. (5 petals)
Fasten off.
Using a yarn sewing needle weave around centre hole to close.
Sew 5 beads into centre of flower.

finishing

Line crochet piece on WS (before sewing seams) – see page 22, Method 2 for lining instructions. With RS of crocheted piece together, fold bottom edge up to 8th row from top of Flap. With RS together, sew side seams of crochet piece. Turn RS out.

Attach snap fastener to WS at end Flap and corresponding place on main piece. Sew crochet flower on RS end of Flap (above snap fastener).

patchwork sewing machine cosy

This is a much nicer cover for your sewing machine than the plastic ones that come with the machine. Customise your own sewing machine by making this Cosy with crochet squares joined together with a double crochet seam. This doesn't need lining, but a lining will prevent the cotton reel holder from poking through the holes of the crochet stitches.

materials

Debbie Bliss Baby Cashmerino, 55% wool/33% acrylic/12% cashmere lightweight DK (sport weight) yarn
2 x 50g (1¾oz) balls - approx. 250m (274yd) - of:
A: 101 (off white)
1 x 50g (1¾oz) ball - approx. 125m (137yd) - each of:
B: 68 Peach Melba (peach)
C: 18 Citrus (green)
D: 83 Butter (yellow)
E: 59 Mallard (teal blue)
F: 202 Light Blue (pale blue)

4mm (US size G/6) crochet hook

½m (½yd) of cotton fabric

tension

Each square measures approx. 10cm (4in), using 4mm (US size G/6) hook and Debbie Bliss Baby Cashmerino yarn.

finished measurement

To fit a standard-sized sewing machine, 40 x 30 x 10cm (16 x 12 x 4in)

abbreviations

approx. approximately
ch chain
ch sp chain space
dc double crochet
htr half treble
rep repeat
RS right side
ss slip stitch
sp(s) space(s)
st(s) stitch(es)
tr treble
WS wrong side

colourway

Make a total of 34 squares in the following colours:
Off white x 5
Peach x 6
Green x 5
Yellow x 6
Teal blue x 5
Pale blue x 7

● ●

squares

Using one colour per square (A, B, C, D, E or F). Make 6ch, join with a ss to form a ring.
Round 1 (RS): 3ch (counts as 1tr), 15tr in ring, join with a ss in top of first 3-ch. (16 sts)
Round 2: 4ch (counts as 1tr, 1ch), [1tr, 1ch] in next st 15 times, join with a ss in third of first 4-ch. (16 tr)
Round 3: 3ch, * 1tr in next ch sp, 1tr in next st; rep from * to end, ending 1tr in last ch sp, join with a ss in top of first 3-ch. (32 tr)

Round 4: 3ch (counts as 1tr), [4tr, 3ch, 5tr] in same place as ss (corner), miss 2 sts, 1dc in next st, 5tr in next st, 1dc in next st, miss 2 sts, *[5tr, 3ch, 5tr] in next st (corner), miss 2 sts, 1dc in next st, 5tr in next st, 1dc in next st, miss 2 sts; rep from * to end, join with a ss in top of first 3-ch.

Round 5: 4ch, miss first 5 tr, 1dc in corner ch sp, 1ch, 1dc in same ch sp, 4ch, miss next 5 tr, 1dc in next dc, 4ch, miss 5 tr, 1dc in next dc, *4ch, miss next 5 tr, 1dc in corner ch sp, 1ch, 1dc in same ch sp, 4ch, miss next 5 tr, 1dc in next dc, 4ch, miss 5 tr, 1dc in next dc; rep from * ending last rep ss in base of first 4-ch.

Round 6: Ss in first ch sp, 2ch (counts as first htr), 4htr in same ch sp, *[3htr, 1ch, 3htr] in next 1ch sp (corner), [5htr in next ch sp] three times; rep from * ending last rep 5htr in each of last 2-ch sps, join with a ss in top of first 2-ch.
Fasten off.

finishing

Block and press Squares lightly.
Lay out the squares with 4 squares across x 3 squares down, placing the colours randomly. With WS together make double crochet seams, joining the squares together into a panel for the front.
Repeat to make a panel for the back.
Make two panels of 3 x 1 squares for the sides.
Make one panel of 4 x 1 squares for the top.

With WS together, join one side of the top to the front and the other side to the back.
With WS together, add the first side panel, starting at the bottom edge of the front, along top edge and down back edge.
Repeat on other side.

Make up a lining in cotton fabric (see page 22, Method 1). Insert the lining into the Cosy with WS together. Turn over the hem of the lining at the bottom edge and pin in place around the edge of the crochet piece. Machine stitch or hand sew edge in place.

colouring pencil cosies

These look very cute in an office pen pot or as a gift for a child. The pencil cosy is a nice introduction to crocheting spirals in the round. These flowers are for the more experienced crocheter, but any flower will look just as good.

materials

Debbie Bliss Baby Cashmerino, 55% wool/33% acrylic/ 12% cashmere lightweight DK (sport weight) yarn
1 x 50g (1¾oz) ball - approx. 125m (137yd) - each of:

cosies
A: 02 Apple (green)
B: 68 Peach Melba (peach)
C: 01 Primrose (yellow)
D: 204 Baby Blue (blue)
E: 06 Candy Pink (pink)

flowers
E: 06 Candy Pink (pink)
F: 97 Speedwell (lilac)
G: 01 Primrose (yellow)
H: 68 Peach Melba (peach)

2.5mm (US size C/2) crochet hook

tension

Tension is not important in this project.

finished measurement

Approx. length of a pencil: 17cm (6½in)

abbreviations

approx. approximate(ly)
ch chain
dc double crochet
rep repeat
ss slip stitch
st(s) stitch(es)
tr treble
WS wrong side

special abbreviation

Picot - 3ch, ss in first of 3-ch.

• •

cosy

(make 1 per pencil)
Using A, B, C, D , E or F, make 2ch, 8dc in second ch from hook.
Work in a spiral making 1dc in each st until work measures 17cm (6½in) or to length of pencil.
Fasten off.
Using a yarn sewing needle sew the first end closed.

flowers

(make 1 flower per cosy)
rose:
Using any Flower colour yarn, make 36ch.
Round 1 (RS): 1tr in fourth ch from hook, [3ch, ss in first of 3-ch] (picot made), [1tr in same ch as previous tr made, 1 picot] twice, *1dc in next ch, 1 picot, [1tr in next ch, 1 picot] five times; rep from * once more. [1dc in next ch, 5tr in next ch] seven times, [1dc in next ch, 1tr, 1ch, 1tr in next ch] three times.
Fasten off leaving a long tail.
With WS facing, roll petals starting from the end of first petal and keeping the base level, pin in place and with a yarn sewing needle thread end and sew through base of petals several times to secure.

marigold:

Using any Flower colour yarn, make 4ch, join with a ss to form a ring.

Round 1: 2ch (counts as first dc), 9dc in ring, ss in top of first 2ch. (10 sts)

Round 2: [5ch, ss in 2nd ch from hook and each of following 3-ch, ss in front strand only of next st] ten times. (10 petals)

Round 3: Bend petals forward and work into the remaining back loop of each st of first round. 2ch (counts as first dc), ss in first st, 1dc in each of next 9 sts, ss in top of first 2ch. (10 sts)

Round 4: [5ch, ss in 2nd ch from hook and each of following 3ch, ss in front strand only of st below, ss in front strand of the next st] ten times. (10 petals)

Round 5: Work as Round 3. (10 petals)

Round 6: Rep Round 4.
Fasten off.
Sew in ends.

finishing

Sew a Flower onto closed end of each pencil Cosy, and then slip Cosy onto a pencil.

cutlery cosies

Crochet for the table! Great for individual place settings and also a really good way to start learning how to bead.

materials

DMC Natura Just Cotton, 100% cotton 4ply yarn
1 x 50g (1¾oz) ball – approx. 155m (169yd) per ball – of:
N03 Sable (light grey)

3.5mm (US size E/4) crochet hook

Approx. 114 size 6 pale pink seed beads for each cosy

tension

approx. 20 sts x 22 rows over a 10cm (4in) square, working double crochet using 3.5mm (US size E/4) hook and Natura Just Cotton yarn.

finished measurement

Approx. 10cm (4in) wide x 11.5cm (4½in) long

note

The multiple is any number of sts (+ 1 for the base ch) (see page 18).

abbreviations

approx. approximate(ly)
ch chain
dc double crochet
rep repeat
RS right side
st(s) stitch(es)

special abbreviation

PB place bead – *On a WS row, insert hook in next dc, yrh, pull yarn through (2 loops now on hook), slide bead up close to work, yrh, pull yarn through both loops on hook to complete beaded dc.*

. . . .

front

Thread approx. 114 beads onto yarn (see page 19).
Make 21ch.
Row 1 (RS): 1dc in second ch from hook, 1dc in each st to end. (20 sts)
Row 2: 1ch, 1dc in first st, *1dc/pb in next st, 1dc in next st; rep from * to last 2 sts, 1dc in each of last 2 sts. (20 sts)
Row 3: 1ch, 1dc in each st to end. (20 sts)
Row 4: 1ch, 1dc/pb in first st, 1dc in next st, *1dc/pb in next st, 1dc in next st; rep from * to end. (20 sts)
Row 5: Rep Row 3.
Rep rows 2–5 until 25 rows have been worked or work measures approx. 11.5cm (4½in.)
Fasten off.

back

Make 21ch.
Row 1 (RS): 1dc in second ch from hook, 1dc in each st to end. (20 sts)
Row 2: 1ch, 1dc in each st to end. (20 sts)
Rep Row 2 until 25 rows have been worked or work measures approx. 11.5cm (4½in).
Fasten off.

finishing

Sew in ends. Place Front and Back with RS together. Sew side and bottom seams.
Turn RS out.

diary cosy

A great little cosy for keeping all your secrets safe. This fits a 2-page a day A5 diary, but would also fit an A5 one-page a day diary.

materials

cosy
Louisa Harding Cassia, 75% superwash wool/25% nylon DK weight yarn
1 x 50g (1¾oz) ball – approx. 132m (144yd) – each of:
A: 103 Chick (yellow)
B: 105 Glacier (blue)

hearts
Debbie Bliss Rialto DK, 100% merino wool DK weight yarn
1 x 50g (1¾oz) ball – approx. 105m (115yd) – of:
C: 12 Scarlet (red)

bookmark
DMC Natura Just Cotton, 100% cotton 4ply yarn
1 x 50g (1¾oz) ball – approx. 155m (169yd) per ball – of:
D: 03 Sable (light grey)

3.5mm (US size E/4) crochet hook

Approx. 39 size 6 pale pink seed beads

tension
7 shell patts x 12 rows over 10cm (4in) square, using 3.5mm (US size E/4) hook and Louisa Harding Cassia yarn.

finished measurement
26 x 16.5 x 2.5cm (9 x 6½ x 1in)

abbreviations

approx. approximately
ch chain
ch sp chain space
dc double crochet
dtr double treble
htr half treble
patt(s) pattern(s)
rep repeat
RS right side
ss slip stitch
st(s) stitch(es)
tr treble
WS wrong side

The multiple is 3 sts + 2 sts (+ 1 for the base ch) (see page 18).

back

(working from top to bottom)
Using A, make 36ch.

top edging:

Row 1: 1dc in second ch from hook, 1dc in each ch to end. (35 sts)
Cut yarn, do not fasten off.
Row 2 (WS): Join B, 2ch, miss first st *[1dc, 2ch, 1dc] in next st, miss next 2 sts; rep from * to end, 1htr in 1-ch from Row 1.
Row 3 (RS): 3ch, *3tr in next 2-ch sp (shell made); rep from * to last st, 1tr in top of first 2-ch from previous row. (11 shells made)
Row 4: 2ch, *[1dc, 2ch, 1dc] in second tr of next shell; rep from * to last st, 1htr in top of first 3-ch from previous row.
Rep Rows 3–4 until 25 rows are worked or work measures 23cm (9in), ending on a Row 4.
Cut yarn, do not fasten off.

bottom edging:

Row 1: Join A, 1ch, 1dc in each of first 2 sts, *1dc in 2-ch sp, 1dc in each of next 2 sts; rep from * to end, ending, 1dc in top of 3-ch from previous row. (35 sts)
Row 2: 1ch, working in front loop of sts only, 1dc in each st to end. (35 sts)
Row 3: 1ch, working in back loop of sts only, 1dc in each st to end. (35 sts)
Row 4: 1ch, working in both loops of sts, 1dc in each st to end. (35 sts)
Row 5: Rep Row 4.
Row 6: 1ch, working in front loop of sts only, 1dc in each st to end. (35 sts)
Row 7: 1ch, working in back loop of sts only, 1dc in each st to end. (35 sts)
Row 8: 1ch, working in both loops of sts, 1dc in each st to end. (35 sts)
Fasten off.

front

(working from bottom to top)

Row 1 (WS): Join B in first 1ch of Row 8. 2ch, miss 2 sts, *[1dc, 2ch, 1dc] in next st, miss next 2 sts; rep from * to end, 1htr in first 1-ch from previous row.

Row 2 (RS): 3ch, *3tr in next 2-ch sp (shell made); rep from * to last st, 1tr in top of first 2-ch from previous row.

Row 3: 2ch, *[1dc, 2ch, 1dc] in second tr of next shell; rep from * to last st, 1htr in top of first 3-ch from previous row. (11 shells made)

Rep Rows 2–3 until 25 rows have been worked or work measures 23cm (9in), ending on a Row 3.

Cut yarn, do not fasten off.

top edging:

Row 1 (RS): Join A, 1ch, 1dc in each of first 2 sts, *1dc in 2-ch sp, 1dc in each of next 2 sts; rep from * to last st, 1dc in last st, 1dc in top of 3-ch from previous row. (35 sts)

Row 2: Ss in each st to end.

Do not fasten off.

spine side 1:

With WS facing and working down first side.

Row 1: 1ch, 1dc in side of last row just made. Make approx. 37dc evenly to first ridge of bottom edge, 2dc in edge of ridge, 2dc along base to next ridge, 2dc in edge of next ridge, make approx. 37dc evenly from bottom of top of Back edging.

Row 2: 1ch, 1dc in back loop of each st to end.

Row 3: 1ch, 1dc in both loops of each st to end.

Do not fasten off.

Fold with WS together so double crochet seam is visible on RS.

Pin seam together starting by matching the bottom edges, 1ch, join using a double crochet seam.

Fasten off.

spine side 2:

With WS facing, join yarn in top of Back edge.

Repeat Spine Side 1.

finishing

Sew in ends.

Block and press on WS.

heart

(make 2)

Using C, make 4ch, join with a ss to form a ring.

Round 1: 3ch, [3dtr, 3tr] into ring, [1ch, 1dtr, 1ch] into ring, [3tr, 3dtr] into ring, 3ch, join with a ss in ring.

Fasten off.

Sew one Heart in centre of Front.

bookmark

Thread beads onto yarn D, make a chain approx. 34cm (13½in) long, incorporating a bead on every alternate chain made. Sew second Heart onto one end.

suppliers

UK STOCKISTS

Deramores
(yarn, crochet hooks, accessories)
0800 488 0708 or 01795 668144
www.deramores.com
customer.service@deramores.com

Designer Yarns
(distributor for Debbie Bliss yarns)
www.designeryarns.uk.com

Fyberspates Ltd
(yarn, crochet hooks)
01829 732525
fyberspates@btinternet.com
www.fyberspates.co.uk

Hobbycraft
(yarn, crochet hooks)
Stores nationwide
0330 026 1400
www.hobbycraft.co.uk

Laughing Hens
(yarn, accessories)
The Croft Stables
Station Lane
Great Barrow
Cheshire CH3 7JN
01829 740903
www.laughinghens.com
sales@laughinghens.com

John Lewis
(yarn, crochet hooks, accessories)
Stores nationwide
03456 049049 or 01698 545454
www.johnlewis.com

TUITION

Nicki Trench
Crochet Club, workshops, accessories
www.nickitrench.com
nicki@nickitrench.com

ACCESSORIES

Addi Needles
(crochet hooks)
01529 240510
www.addineedles.co.uk
addineedles@yahoo.co.uk

Debbie Abrahams Beads
(beads)
0115 855 1799
www.debbieabrahamsbeads.co.uk
beads@debbieabrahamsbeads.com

Knit Pro
(crochet hooks)
www.knitpro.eu

US STOCKISTS

Knitting Fever
(Debbie Bliss, Noro and Sirdar yarns)
Stores nationwide
www.knittingfever.com

The Knitting Garden
(Debbie Bliss, Noro and Sirdar yarns)
www.theknittinggarden.org

Webs
(yarn, crochet hooks, accessories, tuition)
75 Service Center Rd
Northampton, MA 01060
1-800-367-9327
www.yarn.com
customerservice@yarn.com

ACCESSORIES

A.C. Moore
(crochet hooks, accessories)
Online and east coast stores
1-888-226-6673
www.acmoore.com

Hobby Lobby
(crochet hooks, accessories)
Online and stores nationwide
1-800-888-0321
www.hobbylobby.com

Jo-Ann Fabric and Craft Store
(crochet hooks, accessories)
Stores nationwide
1-888-739-4120
www.joann.com

Michaels
(crochet hooks, beads)
Stores nationwide
1-800-642-4235
www.michaels.com

Unicorn Books and Crafts
(crochet hooks, accessories)
1-707-762-3362
www.unicornbooks.com
help@unicornbooks.com

index

acknowledgements

It's impossible to produce a book like this without a fantastic group of people around me. Working on this project has been a great pleasure and I would like to say a big thank you to Anna Galkina from CICO Books who has been a joy to work with. Also a big thank you to Cindy Richards from CICO, who had the faith and confidence to commission me to work on this lovely book.

I am forever grateful and much appreciate all the help I have from my makers: Carolyn Meggison, Jenny Shore and Sian Warr for their diligence, good humour and attention to detail, thanks also to Paula Watkins for her great embroidery skills; to Jean Burden for the gorgeous Dorset button on the Kindle Cosy and to my mum for working through my patterns and crocheting some of the projects.

There are also thanks needed to the editors and checkers; Marie Clayton who edits most of my books and as always, worked on this with great insight and efficiency and also to Jane Czaja, the best pattern checker ever. Thanks also to Sally Powell at CICO, photographer Gavin Kingcome, stylists Sophie Martell and Nel Haynes, and to Barbara Zuniga for the book design.

I have used all my favourite yarns in this book and I'm very grateful to Rhiannon, Nicole and Graeme at Designer Yarns for sending me the yarns so quickly and efficiently and also to Jeni at Fyberspates for letting me use her gorgeous Scrumptious yarn.

On a personal note, I would like to thank all my family for being so willing to get involved in the creative process and lending their honest opinions on the projects as they emerged. Thanks also to Victoria Solomon for her help before the project got started. And last but most certainly not least, a heart-felt thank you to JK for stepping in and kicking me into gear with an incredible amount of support and strength.